Twayne's English Authors Series

Sylvia E. Bowman, *Editor*

INDIANA UNIVERSITY

James Clarence Mangan

 171

James Clarence Mangan

James Clarence Mangan

By HENRY J. DONAGHY

Idaho State University

Twayne Publishers, Inc. :: New York

Library of Congress Cataloging in Publication Data

Donaghy, Henry J
  James Clarence Mangan.

  (Twayne's English authors series, TEAS 171)
  Bibliography: p. 134.
  1. Mangan, James Clarence, 1803-1849.
PR4973.Z5D6   821'.8   74-6270
ISBN 0-8057-1370-0

PR
4973
.Z5D6

66757

To My Mother
Catherine McQuaid Donaghy

Preface

A century and a half of Irish poetry exists between Oliver Goldsmith and William Butler Yeats that is virtually unknown. The average reader is totally unfamiliar with the names chronicled in the history of this period. The name of Tom Moore may be an exception; but, if so, it is remembered more because of Moore's friendship with Byron than because of the appeal of his poetry to today's reader. The purpose of this book is not, of course, to examine in any detail Irish poetry of the late eighteenth and nineteenth centuries; it is to take the most gifted poet of that period — James Clarence Mangan — and help the reader become somewhat more familiar with his life and work.

James Clarence Mangan is an Irish Romantic poet of the early nineteenth century. If he is not well known to students of British Romantic poetry, it may be because recent anthologies of Romanticism, like David Perkins's fine text, have concentrated on giving more complete selections from the major poets. Nevertheless, Mangan is sufficiently important for Russell Noyes to have included in his anthology of English Romanticism. Oliver Elton insists that Mangan's truly good work is limited but that it is very good indeed. Albert Baugh's history places him at the head of the Young Ireland group of whom Yeats edited an anthology; and, most recently, W. H. Auden included him in his anthology of nineteenth-century poets.

Despite these token indications of Mangan's importance, most popular editions of nineteenth-century poets have failed to include some of the greatest triumphs of Mangan, and too many have merely passed judgment about some popular favorites, such as his "Dark Rosaleen."

Mangan, a fascinating poet, has been called the "Irish Poe" because the two contemporaries are so very similar in their lives and in their poetic styles. Both suffered from unrequited love, both were morbidly melancholic, both turned to alcohol and probably drugs, both had difficulty holding jobs because of their indulgence, and both died in the same year, victims of their indulgences. However, not their lives but their styles link them in the minds of most critics. Poe's peculiar use of rhythm and refrain, as well as incremental repetition and internal rhyme, were used by Mangan before him. This priority of Mangan has led to assertions about Mangan's influence on Poe, but such claims are at best dubious.

A more evident and important influence is that which Mangan exerted on his fellow Irishmen James Joyce and Yeats. Joyce, who wrote and spoke of Mangan with almost apostolic fervor, considered him to be Poe's superior if not his master. This praise cannot be attributed merely to nationalism because Joyce was notoriously apolitical and unnationalistic; in fact, he was critical of Mangan only for being too much so. More important, however, is Mangan's influence on Yeats and the modern Irish Renaissance. Mangan was the leader of the Young Ireland group, the group which began the Irish literary rebirth that came to fruition in the twentieth century. Yeats was early influenced by the Young Ireland poets, edited an anthology of Young Ireland verse, wrote a couple of articles on Mangan, and showed the influence of Mangan in his verse.

The Irish Renaissance was not something that sprang spontaneously to life with Yeats and the Abbey Theatre; rather it began with renewed interest in Gaelic studies earlier in the nineteenth century. Mangan was the poet who par excellence made the ancient Gaelic bards come to new life. As such, one could argue that Mangan was the father of the later Irish literary revival. However, this work deals not only with Mangan's place of influence in later Irish letters but also — and primarily — with the poet's own importance. Of Mangan's eight hundred or more poems,[1] most are ephemeral, topical pieces, but he wrote thirty or forty poems of real and lasting quality. In my opinion, the student of nineteenth-century Romanticism, or of any other movement, will find more in the first-rate work of minor writers than he will in the second- or third-rate work of the major poets.

This book studies not only Mangan's better known works but also his lesser known ones of genuine merit. It considers the important question of the extent to which Mangan "translated" or created; and it studies very briefly Mangan's prose works, though most of these are ephemeral. Finally, it discusses the influence of Mangan on Joyce, Yeats, Poe, and others in order to provide a more complete consideration of his importance and of his place in the tradition of Irish letters which has come to such fruition in this century.

Since there is no edition of Mangan's poems in print, this text has in many instances reproduced the full poem under consideration. I would like to take space here to thank Professor James MacKillop, whose knowledge of Mangan and whose bibliographical leads were a great help to me. Also, I owe a debt of thanks to Mr. Terry Lynch, whose spadework was both helpful and encouraging. Finally, I am most grateful to my wife, Joyce, for her patient rereading of the text.

HENRY J. DONAGHY

Idaho State University

Contents

Preface

Chronology

1. The Life of James Clarence Mangan   15
2. German and Oriental "Translations"   29
3. Irish Poems   60
4. Original Poems   97
5. Prose Works   119
6. Influence on Other Writers   122

Notes and References   130

Selected Bibliography   134

Index   139

Chronology

1803   James Mangan born May 1 on Fishamble Street, Dublin, in same year as Thomas Lovell Beddoes (they die same year also); James is first son of a teacher turned grocer.

1808   Brother William born; girl tells James rain will make him grow; he goes out in it, and excessive exposure (Mangan tells us) causes serious blindness for eight years.

1810   Placed in school in Saul's Court; Father Graham gives him groundwork in Latin, French, Italian, and Spanish; "nearest relations" think youngster mad.

1818   Becomes breadwinner of family when sent by father to work in scrivener's office; earliest poems appear in almanacs.

1826   On stimulants already; writes little; reads occult works.

1831   Reads Swedenborg; becomes member of "Comet Club" fighting English tithes for Protestant clergy, many of whom are absentees.

1832   "Elegiac Verses on Death of a Beloved Friend" written for his student, Catherine Hayes.

1833   Indulges in opium; end of love relationship with Margaret Stackpoole; hint of disappointed love in subsequent poetry.

1834   *Dublin University Magazine,* best literary organ in Ireland, begun; Mangan contributes, giving up work as scrivener.

1837   First of his "Literae Orientales" for *Dublin University Magazine* and heavy contribution of "translations" follows to this journal.

1838   Becomes copier for Ordnance Survey; transcribes documents at Trinity College to help support relatives.

1840   Best work begins to appear: "Woman of Three Cows," "Twenty Golden Years Ago," "O'Hussey's Ode to the Maguire," and "Lament for the Princes of Tyrone and Tyrconnell."

1841   Produces couple of unsigned papers on "German Ghosts and Ghost Seers"; begins to disappear from society and to return after long absences.

1842   First number of *The Nation,* political organ for Young Ireland; Mangan's work for the magazine not political or nationalistic at this time.

1844   Produces "The Karamanian Exile" and other Ottoman poetry; begins work as assistant cataloguer for Trinity College Library.

1845   *Anthologia Germanica* brought out, not best Mangan but German "translations" appeal to Henry Wadsworth Longfellow.

1846   Contributes largely to *The Nation* with work like "Dark Rosaleen"; now becomes national poet of Ireland.

1848   Becomes very ill and is sent to St. Vincent's Hospital, gets up and leaves while weak and falls into foundation of a new building in an unfamiliar neighborhood.

1849   Found dying in wretchedness in a Bride Street cellar after having left a temporary shelter for cholera, an aftermath of the famine; dies on June 20 in Meath Hospital of cholera or starvation; buried at Glasnevin Cemetery with a virtually unattended funeral.

CHAPTER 1

The Life of
James Clarence Mangan

JAMES Clarence Mangan was born on May 1, 1803, the year that "Bold" Robert Emmet was hanged for his Dublin Revolt. The future poet's father, James Mangan, who was born in Shanagolden, County Limerick, had been a schoolteacher; but he had turned grocer because a grocery business had been inherited by his wife. Mangan's mother came from Kiltale, County Meath; and her first child, the future poet, was born in the house she had inherited with the grocery. The house, Number 3 Fishamble Street, Dublin, was a dingy, four-storied building; and three other children, two boys and a girl, were born there. All the children seem to have found their mother kind and sympathetic, but James found his father to be a source of suffering. An improvident businessman, the elder Mangan eventually went bankrupt; but he was carefree and seems to have been more interested in the jovial companionship of his peers than in the sensitive nature of his son.[1]

I Family Life and Education

Mangan goes into some detail about his father in his fragmentary *Autobiography:*

His temper was not merely quick and irascible, but it also embodied much of that calm concentrated spirit of Milesian fierceness, a picture of which I have endeavoured to paint in my Italian story of "Gasparo Bandollo." His nature was truly noble; to quote a phrase of my friend O'Donovan, he "never knew what it was to refuse the countenance of living man" — but, in neglecting his own interests — and not the most selfish of misanthropes could accuse him of attending too closely to those — he unfortunately forgot the injuries that he inflicted upon the interests of others. He was of an ardent and forward-bounding disposition, and, though deeply religious by nature, he hated the restraints of social life, and seemed to think that all feelings with regard to family connections, and the obligations imposed by them, were totally beneath his notice. Me, my two brothers, and my sister, he treated habitually as a huntsman would treat refractory hounds. It was his boast, uttered in pure glee of heart, that we "would run into a mouse-hole" to shun him. While my mother lived he made her miserable — he led my only sister such a life that she was obliged to leave our house — he kept up a succession of hostilities with my brothers — and if he spared me more than others it was perhaps because I displayed a greater contempt of life and everything connected with it than he thought was shown by the other members of his family. If any one can imagine such an idea as a human boa-constrictor *without his alimentive propensities* he will be able to form some notion of the character of my father. May GOD assoil his great and mistaken soul and grant him eternal peace and forgiveness! — but I have an inward feeling that to him I owe all my misfortunes.[2]

To what extent we can trust Mangan's somewhat self-pitying autobiography is difficult to say. D. J. O'Donoghue, Mangan's best biographer, is too cavalier about it. On the other hand, Mangan admits to dreaming about matters he writes of as objective reality; for, when Father Meehan, Mangan's friend in later years, questioned his description of an early home in the *Autobiography,* Mangan said, "I dreamt it."[3] Rather than discredit much of what Mangan says, James Joyce's more sensitive interpretation should be heeded:

"May be I dreamed it." The world, you see, has become somewhat unreal for him, and he has begun to contemn that which is, in fine, the occasion of much error. How will it be with those dreams which, for every young and simple heart, take such dear reality upon themselves? One whose nature is so sensitive cannot forget his dreams in a secure, strenuous life. He doubts them, and puts them from him for a time, but when he hears men denying them with an oath he would acknowledge them proudly, and where sensitiveness has induced weakness, or, as here, refined upon natural weakness, would even compromise with the world, and win from it in return the favour of silence, if no more, as for that desire of the heart so loudly derided, that rudely entreated idea. His manner is such that none can say if it be pride or humility that looks out of that vague face, which seems to live only because of those light shining eyes and of the fair silken hair above it, of which he is not a little vain.[4]

Mangan's schooling was brief. He attended an academy in Saul's Court when seven years of age; but after a few years he was transferred to a school in Derby Square because of his father's financial embarrassment. This school was run by his former teacher at Saul's Court, Michael Courtney; and, after some time there, Mangan came under the instruction of Father Graham, a priest to whom he owed his foundation in Latin, French, Spanish, and Italian.

Then his father in 1818, having failed in eight successive establishments, Mangan tells us, asked his oldest son to be the family breadwinner; and thus began, according to what Mangan tells us, the worst years of his life:

I was fifteen years old; could I not even then begin to exert myself for the behoof of my kindred? If my excellent mother thought so, she said nothing, but my father undertook the solution of the question; and I was apprenticed to a scrivener. Taken from my books — obliged to relinquish my solitary rambles and musings — and compelled, for the miserable pittance of a few shillings weekly, to herd with the coarsest of associates and suffer at their hands every sort of rudeness and indignity which their uncultivated and semi-savage natures prompted them to inflict on me: "Thus bad begun, but worse remained behind."[5]

II   *The Scrivener's Office and Poetic Apprenticeship*

This period of work in the scrivener's office created a trauma in Mangan's life to which he constantly alluded, even on his deathbed, as one of the major sources of his sickness of body and soul. O'Donoghue, who dismisses Mangan's account of this period, remarks that he must have confused it with his later period of employment in a law office. And later critics, like A. P. Graves in a *Cornhill Magazine* article entitled "James Clarence Mangan" (1898), have accepted what O'Donoghue "proves." However, O'Donoghue's account is nothing more than hypothesis. The only "proof" he advances is that the business was being conducted by Father Kenrick for his widowed sister-in-law; and the two Kenrick boys, who later became American archbishops in Baltimore and St. Louis, also worked there for their uncle. Thus, concludes O'Donoghue, the environment could not have been the one described by Mangan.

The proper interpretation is that Mangan probably suffered what he has described in the *Autobiography* and elsewhere, whether or not someone else finds that Mangan accurately described the environment of the scrivener's office. James Joyce's approach to Mangan's description of his father might well be applied to all of the instances where Mangan describes sufferings for which others cannot find an objective basis in reality. Joyce points out that, amid the defenses and condemnations of Mangan's father, we overlook "how keenly a sensitive boy suffers from contact with a gross nature."[6]

Mangan worked seven years in this scrivener's office, and then was employed in various attorneys' offices, doing scrivenery work, until 1834. He started publishing poetry in 1818 when he began work at the scrivener's. Most of these early poems are callow, whimsical pieces which he published in various magazines, such as the *New Ladies Almanack*. Ironically, Mangan produced many humorous pieces during this traumatic period; and Desmond Sheridan may be correct in saying that Mangan should have purged his feelings more as he did in "Genius." But we cannot understand Mangan fully without understanding the genuinely humorous side of a personality that was so often plunged in melancholy; for, when we do, we cannot lament the wasting of his genius on humor that was "unnatural" to him. Furthermore, some of Mangan's finest work, like "Twenty Golden Years Ago," shows that older Irish tradition of moving from the serious literary form to the grotesquely humorous and back again, as G. K. Chesterton has aptly pointed out.[7]

During this period of his poetic apprenticeship, between 1818 and 1826, Mangan tells us that he returned from the drudgery of the office to a dismal home that was without parallel in the cities of Europe — an account that, as we have seen, Father Meehan did not believe. O'Donoghue also questions Mangan when he tells us that he worked so hard and so long that he returned home from the office between eleven and twelve each night. Whatever time Mangan returned from Kenrick's, his only recreation seems to have been reading, which damaged his eyes, the recitation aloud of passages from Shakespeare and from Byron, both of whom he committed largely to memory, and the writing of verse. During these years, Mangan seems to have begun taking opium, a habit which he denied with such vehemence to Gavan Duffy that Duffy instantly believed his denial. Yet Duffy's reason for belief seems contradictory. He had been warning Mangan against what had happened to Samuel Taylor Coleridge; and, when Mangan denied the habit, Duffy seemed to think he would not be so ashamed of a habit shared by Thomas De Quincey and Coleridge![8]

There seems little doubt that Mangan took opium. His biographers are convinced of it, as was the majority of his associates during his lifetime. O'Donoghue uses his prose work, "An Extraordinary Adventure in the Shades" that was written for *The Comet* in 1833, to show not only that Mangan was taking opium but also that he did so under the influence of Thomas De Quincey.[9] Louise Imogen Guiney points out that Mangan "was going the dark way of the opium-eater," yet was mistakenly called a drunkard.[10] And John

Mitchel, his first biographer, describes Mangan while the poet was working to support his family as "the bond slave of opium."[11]

Mangan probably took opium because he was depressed about his need to work at Kenrick's, because of loneliness, and because he was suffering from physical illness. His melancholy was increased by his being required at a tender age to support his whole family, including a sick brother. Furthermore, he had from adolescence a Romantic sense of isolation that developed to the verge of sickness:

I loved to indulge in solitary rhapsodies, and, if intruded on upon those occasions, I was made very unhappy. Yet I had none of the ordinary shyness of boyhood. I merely felt or fancied that between me and those who approached me, no species of sympathy could exist; and I shrank from communion with them as from somewhat alien from my nature. This feeling continued to acquire strength daily, until in after years it became one of the grand and terrible miseries of my existence. It was a morbid product of the pride and presumption which, almost hidden from myself, constituted even from my childhood governing traits in my character, and have so often rendered me repulsive in the eyes of others.[12]

Mangan's physical ailment may have been caused by a childhood prank, for he tells us in another autobiographical fragment related in the third person that "a hare-brained girl who lodged in his father's house, sent him out one day to buy a ballad; he had no covering on his head, and there was a tremendous shower of rain: but she told him the rain would make him grow. He believed her, went out, strayed through many streets and bye-places now abolished, found, at length, his way homeward, and for eight years afterwards, from his fifth year to his thirteenth, remained almost blind. In the twilight alone could he attempt to open his eyes, and then he — read."[13]

Whatever caused Mangan's ailment, he may have begun taking opium to relieve this physical illness. Opium was a habit he seemed to indulge in until the early 1830's; but, when he managed to cease, he used alcohol as a temporary crutch; and it became a permanent substitute.[14] Throughout these years, however, Mangan's verse gave little indication of his suffering.

III *End of a Poet's Apprenticeship*

About 1827, Mangan's poetic apprenticeship ceased. He contributed little to the almanacs, however, for the next two years.[15] He had begun to work for the attorney's office about 1826; and, once again, he complained of the companions with whom he had to work.

In his spare time he seems to have read only books concerned with the mysterious — reading that later led to a more profound interest in things religious. Mangan was a Roman Catholic though he seems to have been little concerned with formal religion during his middle years. Certainly he was not the pious Catholic or faithful communicant some have presented him as being.[16]

O'Donoghue himself stresses the "faithful Catholic" theme too much; and he fails, as a result, to give due credit to the Spiritualist and Swedenborgian strains in the poet. We do not imply (as will be made clear later) that Mangan's poetry was ever seriously influenced by Swedenborg as was William Blake's. But during his thirties, his personal life seems to have been a religiously eclectic one, and his personal search, though it did not manifest itself in his Oriental "translations," which occupied most of these years, did show itself to some extent in his original works. The Mangan who wrote "The One Mystery" in 1833 was, as will be seen when we treat that poem, a kind of Shelleyan skeptic about the ability of religion to offer any answers to life's fundamental problems. By 1840, when he wrote "Life and Its Illusions," he has a definite belief in a First Cause and perhaps a belief in a life hereafter as a reward for those who have lived virtuously, though he does not view the world in a very "Catholic" or sacramental way.

Mangan did die in the arms of Rome, and he may have been a practicing Catholic in the latter years of his life; but what brought him back to the Catholic Church, besides a close friendship with Father Meehan, was his interest in the mysterious and exotic in art and life — an interest akin to that which brought his later follower, Lionel Johnson, and so many fin-de-siècle writers, like Oscar Wilde and Aubrey Beardsley, into the Church. Mangan tells us in his autobiography: "If I persued [sic] any books with a feeling of pleasure, they were such as treated of the wonderful and terrible in art, nature and society. Descriptions of battles and histories of revolutions; accounts of earthquakes, inundations and tempests; and narratives of 'moving accidents by flood and field,' possessed a charm for me which I could neither resist nor explain. It was some time before this feeling merged altogether into another — the sentiment of religion and its ineffable mysteries."[17]

While Mangan's religious search was occurring, his literary pursuits brought him into contact with the "Comet Club." About 1830 he joined this talented club which comprised the staff of The Comet and whose members included Dr. George Petrie, Eugene O'Curry, and John O'Donovan. The last two men, employed by Petrie, were the two finest Irish scholars of the age; and the collaboration of this threesome "marks the beginning of Modern Gaelic scholarship."[18] When these men became good friends of Mangan, his happiest period began; and, had he enjoyed their friendship earlier, he might not have resorted to opium.

As writers, the staff of *The Comet* was comprised of young satirists bent on doing something about the tithes that Irishmen, regardless of whether they were Catholic or Protestant, had to pay to Protestant clergy of the established Anglican Church, many of whom were absentees. The efforts of *The Comet* lasted until 1833 when the members of the staff were prosecuted by the English government. Mangan's best work was not done, however, for *The Comet*. He wrote much nonsense verse for it and prose in a style imitative of William Maginn, a classics teacher from Cork, who had written parody and banter for *Blackwood's Magazine.*

In 1832, Catherine Hayes, a close friend to whom Mangan was teaching German, died. By his storytelling, he had for a time played Othello to her Desdemona. It may not have been a genuine love affair, or at any rate not the one which caused the poet so much anguish. Catherine Hayes, who was just seventeen when she died, had loved to listen to the stories of Mangan who was, with a captive audience, a raconteur in the style of Coleridge. They also exchanged poems, and Mangan was very much shaken by her untimely death. His "Elegiac Verses on the Death of a Beloved Friend" commemorated the event in *The Comet*.

IV   *Unrequited Love*

The real love of Mangan's life seems to have been Margaret Stackpoole, but the extent to which the termination of the affair affected the poet is uncertain. Mitchel advocates that this disappointment in love had a traumatic effect on Mangan:

He was on terms of visiting in a house where were three sisters; one of them beautiful, spirituelle, and a coquette. The old story was here once more re-enacted in due order. Paradise opened before him; the imaginative and passionate soul of a devoted boy bended in homage before an enchantress. She received it, was pleased with it, even encouraged and stimulated it, by various arts known to that class of persons, until she was fully and proudly conscious of her absolute power over one other gifted and noble nature — until she knew that she was the centre of the whole orbit of his being, and the light of his life; then with a cold surprise, as wondering that he could be guilty of such a foolish presumption, she exercised her undoubted prerogative, and whistled him down the wind. His air paradise was suddenly a darkness and a chaos. . . . He never loved and hardly looked upon any woman for ever more. Neither over his disappointments did he gnash his teeth and beat his breast before the public; nor make himself and his sorrows the burden of his song.[19]

O'Donoghue, who agrees with Mitchel, uses as additional evidence a sketch in *The Dublin Satirist* which he interprets to be autobiographical and from which he decides that Mangan was betrayed by a friend whom he had introduced to Margaret.[20] O'Donoghue also, but very strangely, uses Gavan Duffy as evidence that the Margaret Stackpoole affair "turned the drama of [Mangan's] life into a tragedy"; but Gavan Duffy is responsible for the theory that the Margaret Stackpoole tragedy is greatly exaggerated. Duffy, who was very close to Mangan, says that Mangan told him he was rejected because Margaret, who was living under her maiden name, confessed to Mangan that she was actually married but was waiting for her husband to return from accruing some fortune. Furthermore, the affair, records Duffy, had very little effect on Mangan. Duffy originally told the story to Mitchel who, in the ten years before writing about it, got the facts confused, Duffy remarks. Also, Duffy was the only possible source, the only one who knew of this affair.[21]

Both Louise Imogen Guiney and Desmond Sheridan concur with Duffy, but Sheridan thinks the blow to Mangan was a serious one. Guiney and Duffy are probably correct since Duffy is an original and firsthand source and since Guiney secured her information from Duffy's daughter. O'Donoghue was speculating, and even Mitchel was exercising his imagination. As Guiney observed, "We must remember that a poet's despair cannot gracefully charge itself to dearth of beef, unpleasant kinsfolk, and headaches out of a morphine phial. Hence woman, and the love of woman, come in as the *causa rerum,* irrespective of proof, even with a Mangan."[22]

Whatever the truth of the poet's love for Margaret Stackpoole, we do find an element of disappointment in love in Mangan's later poetry, that written from 1839 on. Sometimes the object of this love is Laura, sometimes Frances; and there is, of course, a possibility that the woman represents Margaret. There is likewise the possibility that Mangan simply presents the common Romantic theme of lost love, previously offered by Goethe, Wordsworth, Chateaubriand, Byron, Shelley, and countless Romantics suffering from *mal de siècle.*

V *Period of "Translations"*

Mangan left *The Comet* before its demise in 1833. He was the butt of jokes on the part of some of the staff, particularly John Sheehan, who ridiculed "Clarence" in print and who finally pushed him beyond endurance by explaining that a piece of Mangan's humor was the work of a drunkard. In 1834, when Mangan stopped working as a scrivener,[23] he began contributing to a new magazine which was to be the finest literary journal in Ireland, the *Dublin University Magazine;* he wrote also for *The Satirist,* and to it he contributed his "translations" from German, something he had begun for *The Comet.* He seems to have lived until 1838 on the small sum he received for such publications.

During these years, Mangan was to write many of his "translations," particularly the first of his "Literae Orientales" in the *Dublin University Magazine.* Thenceforth he provided, especially to the *Dublin University Magazine,* "translations" from Turkish, Arabic, Persian, Welsh, Coptic, Danish, French, Serbian, and Spanish; and he even offered to supply the editor with translations "from the Hindoo." Since a young man could most easily break into a prestigious publication with translations, Mangan used such "translations" as his entrée. Although these translations are discussed in a later chapter, it should be evident to the reader now that the unschooled Mangan was catering to a public taste for exotic translations — a taste which Samuel Taylor Coleridge's German translations, Thomas Moore's *Lalla Rookh,* and the general *weltschmerz* of the age had developed, and upon which Edward FitzGerald's Persian translations would soon capitalize.

Mangan, indeed, did translate some works quite literally, but he added to them the beautiful musical effect peculiar to his poetry. By far the greatest number of his "translations" freely changed the originals and made them into something as personal as did Chaucer the *Decameron* of Boccaccio, or Shakespeare *Holinshed's Chronicles.* Finally, some purported translations were entirely original, but they were attributed to some exotic poet, even to one who did not exist, such as Selber. Since the largest number of Mangan's outstanding poems are "translations," the most immediate influence upon his work is, of course, that of the man he is "translating." However much he failed to understand, however much he changed or improved another writer's work, he seems to have been dependent upon others for suggestion in much of his best work.

Apart from these models, the greatest influence on Mangan appears to have been Lord Byron. Mangan's incredible gift for rhyme came, at least in part, from the author of *Don Juan*, whose works he had committed to memory. The Byronic pose, reflecting the *weltschmerz* of the age, is likewise often found in Mangan. Perhaps just as real but more difficult to establish is the stylistic influence of Coleridge. The experimental rhythms and meter of "Christabel" are seen throughout Mangan's poetry, though they might have been created independently. However, Mangan's "Vision of Connaught in the Thirteenth Century" has obvious stylistic and thematic connections with "Kubla Khan." The influence of Percy Shelley and perhaps William Wordsworth seems evident, especially in so personal a poem as "The One Mystery." The poem's Platonism recalls immediately Wordsworth's "Intimations Ode," as well as Shelley's "Hymn to Intellectual Beauty" and "Epipsychidion," the latter unmistakably in style as well as in idea.

During this period of his "translations," Mangan's drinking became heavy; and he was often found at a corner table of the Phoenix tavern or the Star and Garter. His needs and those of his brother were a constant source of embarrassment to him as he had to beg money from friends — even call on them and find, to his humiliation, that they were entertaining. The poet's appearance at this time offers some idea why people like Sheehan found Mangan ridiculous. He had aged prematurely, and his blond hair was so gray that he self-consciously wore a wig and lied about his age. He was five-feet-six-inches tall and very emaciated. His dentures did not fit, and he was always rearranging them. His threadbare coat was worn in every season and was buttoned to his neck. His shoulders were very narrow, and he compensated by having the coat heavily padded. Often he wore a blue cloak and carried an umbrella under the arm so that the cloak stuck out as though he were carrying bagpipes. On his head, he wore a black, pointed hat, the type commonly associated only with witches. Finally, he wore big, green, eyeglasses which veiled eyes that were as striking as Shelley's.

Mangan exemplified a certain ambivalence between the vulnerable and the aggressive which, however, seems quite common to sensitive souls. On one hand, he lied about his age, wore a wig, and padded his shoulders to cover shortcomings about which he was sensitive. On the other, he flaunted his individuality and eccentricities in an attempt to take pride in the reputation he had developed as an oddity. Like his favorite, Byron, and with perhaps more reason, Mangan seems to have felt his genius was ·unrecognized, to have felt alienated, a "lion among wolves." When he was sixteen, he even wrote in the vein of Byron a very personal poem called "Genius," which we will discuss later.

In 1838, through Dr. Petrie's influence, Mangan was employed by the Ordnance Survey, which required him to go to Marsh's Library, Trinity College, and elsewhere to transcribe documents. Petrie was willing to hire Mangan, despite his undependability, because he had an excellent script from years of serving as a scrivener and because Petrie knew that Mangan could not support his relatives on his earnings from the *Dublin University Magazine.* A very prolific year for Mangan, he produced a number of his Oriental poems and wrote for the *Dublin University Magazine* some of his best prose works, such as "The Thirty Flasks" and "The Man in the Cloak." And in the following year came one of Mangan's best known "translations" from the Arabic, "The Time of the Barmecides." Mangan later improved it by revision, and it seems to have been his favorite among his works. Yet it is indicative of Mangan's humor that he himself wrote the earliest parody of the rhythmic stanzas of this poem.[24]

About this time Mangan became acquainted with the Irish patriot, and leader of Young Ireland, Sir Charles Gavan Duffy, who was at the time editor of the *Belfast Vindicator* and later in 1842 of *The Nation.* Mangan contributed to both, and for a while Gavan Duffy gave him a fixed salary. Though Duffy and Mangan had some trouble because of Mangan's way of life, Duffy was generous, thought highly of Mangan's work, and even defended his political verse, which Louise Imogen Guiney thinks is weak. When Duffy criticized one of Mangan's "translations" by saying it was not Moorish, the poet replied, "Well, never mind, it's Tom Moorish."[25] The pun recalls the poet's reply to Dr. Anster, who tried to show him the disservice he did himself in attributing his own work to others. In particular, the famous translator mentioned Mangan's purported translation of the Persian poet Hafiz, to which Mangan replied, "Hafiz paid better than Mangan — and any critic could see they were only Half-his."[26]

While dealing with Mangan's love of puns and with his attributions of his own works to others, we might mention that, during this year, Mangan also contributed to the *Dublin University Magazine* his Chinese "Elegy on Joe (Tchao) King"; and, in the following year, he attributed one of his finest poems to a German with the fabricated name of "Selber" ("himself"). In this year, 1840, he gave to the *Irish Penny Journal* one of his finest Irish "translations," "Woman of Three Cows," though he knew no Irish at this time. In the same year he also produced two more of his best poems, "O'Hussey's Ode to the Maguire" and "Lament for the Princes of Tyrone and Tyrconnell" — poems that Padraic Colum has considered to be the best of Mangan's Irish poems.

The following year Mangan wrote the poem that Joyce thought truly remarkable, "Kathaleen Ny-Houlahan." The year of 1841 was not a good one for Mangan personally, for he disappeared for weeks at a time, came back, remained completely sober for an interval, and then disappeared again. He made constant vows of repentance, often at the behest of friends; but, struggle as he might, he only stumbled again. The age seems to have known little about the symptoms of alcoholism or drug addiction. Like Coleridge, Mangan would withdraw from laudanum only to take it again when his "illness" appeared. Medical men did not know much about withdrawal symptoms; and, when Mangan experienced such symptoms, the remedy was to turn to the opiate for relief. The vicious cycle ensued.

VI   *The Young Ireland Poet*

In 1842, *The Nation* began publication, and for two or three years Mangan wrote for this organ of "Young Ireland." Young Ireland was a group of patriots and literary men which included — besides the founders of *The Nation*, Thomas Davis, Gavan Duffy, and John Blake — many fine new writers like Speranza (Oscar Wilde's mother), Sir Samuel Fergusson, Richard D'Alton Williams, John O'Connell (son of the great liberator, Daniel O'Connell), and Mangan himself. The group's newfound nationalism brought the Irish back to the literature and traditions of the past; and it was this Young Ireland group that was later to be a strong influence on William Butler Yeats. *The Nation* published the works of these idealists and poets, and Mangan was the finest poet among them. Yet, though Mangan was later to become enthusiastic about the Patriotic cause sponsored by Duffy and Mitchel, he was at this time unnationalistic and apolitical. Indeed, Mangan refused at first to write political verse; but from 1846 on, he became the great national poet and even offered himself to "the cause" in a letter to Duffy.

Duffy kindly refused his services, not only because Mangan would be unreliable but also because radicalism on Mangan's part would jeopardize his post with his conservative employers.

While Mangan wrote light, nonpolitical work for *The Nation* in 1842, he continued for the *Dublin University Magazine* the German translations, which later comprised his collection entitled *Anthologia Germanica*, as well as Oriental and other translations. Perhaps the best German "translations" are those taken from or suggested by Friedrich Rückert. Although "The Ride Around the Parapet" was taken from Rückert's "Die Begrüssung auf dem Kynast," it is far removed from the original poem and constitutes one of Mangan's own finest poems.

In 1844, Mangan seems to have been given a job as an assistant cataloguer in Trinity College Library, which needed him to help prepare a new catalogue. Mangan obtained the position through the influence of his friends, Drs. Anster, Petrie, and particularly Todd. And also through the influence of friends, Mangan's first collection of poetry, the *Anthologia Germanica*, was published. There was a good deal of difficulty achieving publication; indeed, the book only became a reality when Gavan Duffy guaranteed the Dublin publisher, McGlashan, fifty pounds for the first one hundred copies. The book comprised two volumes, containing one hundred and fifty poems; and it seems to have been warmly received. It sold, and the publisher's fears about sales were unnecessary. McGlashan, of course, had not questioned the work's merit, since, as publisher of the *Dublin University Magazine*, he had for some time known and thought highly of Mangan's work. He was a man who seems to have been either parsimonious or excessively paternalistic with the poet, for he very seldom paid his charge in a decent sum and often used the justification that Mangan would only squander a large sum in a hurry.

In 1846 Mangan contributed many poems to *The Nation*, and he now definitely became a national poet, and Ireland's best. The new political influences on Mangan, like those upon other members of Young Ireland, sprang from the revolutionary spirit on the Continent. Especially influential were the Democratic factors which led to the bloodless revolution of 1848 and to the overthrow of Louis Philippe in France, but perhaps even more influential was the less successful nationalism of Mazzini, who gave a prototype to Young Ireland in the formation of his "Young Italy."

To this same year belongs Mangan's most famous work, "Dark

Rosaleen," as well as the very fine poems "The Dream of John Mac Donnell," "A Vision of Connaught in the Thirteenth Century," and "O'Hussey's Ode to the Maguire." Most of his writings after this were, with a few notable exceptions, in the *Dublin University Magazine*.

In 1848 — the same year Duffy, Smith O'Brien, and Mitchel, encouraged by the events in France, led Young Ireland's short-lived revolt against the Government — Mangan became very ill from his mode of life and was confined in May to St. Vincent's Hospital. When he was feeling better, Mangan, a poor patient, got out of bed, put on his clothes, and left. Then, still weak, he fell fifteen feet into the foundations of a building and was confined to Richmond Hospital for a few days. During Mangan's final year, he lived like a tramp. He had no home; and he suffered, as did so many, from the cholera of that year and was admitted to one of the temporary sheds erected to care for the cholera victims. He left this shed at Kilmainham when he became irked by a few days of confinement, and he went to Bride Street where he was found dying in a cellar; whether he was a victim of cholera or of starvation is a moot question. He was taken to Meath Hospital, where he died on June 20, 1849, seven days after his admission. He received the last rites of the Catholic Church and died with the words, "O Mary, Queen of Mercy" on his lips. He was buried at Glasnevin Cemetery on June 23; and his burial ceremony was attended, some say by five; some, three people. Whatever the number or whatever the cause of death, the ending was grim for the finest Irish poet of the time.

CHAPTER 2

German and Oriental "Translations"

M ANGAN'S best known works are his Irish "translations,"
but whether they deserve greater popularity than his
other "translations" or than his original work is questionable since
more truly representative Mangan poems may be found among the
Oriental "translations." And it is more feasible to begin with a consideration of these and of the German translations because the question of whether and to what extent the poems are translations is more
clear-cut in these works.

I *The Translation Question*

While Mangan knew German reasonably well, and came to know
some Irish, he knew nothing of the many Oriental tongues —
Turkish, Persian, Arabic, and Coptic[1] — he chose to "translate"; but
he even offered to supply the editor of the *Dublin University
Magazine* with translations "from the Hindoo." The contemporary
demand for the exotic would have been enough reason for Mangan
to supply these translations; for, as we have observed, such popular
works were an excellent entrée for a young, nameless writer and a
means of publishing more than two or three works in a particular
issue of the *Dublin University Magazine.* Apart from these factors,
Mangan seems to have used the Oriental atmosphere as a
thinly veiled, somber reflection on Ireland's state of soul:

> Then was the Season when Hope was yet glowing,
> Then the blithe year of the Spring and the Sowing;
> Then the Soul dwelt in her own fairy clime;
>   Then was the time,
> Then the gay Time *ere* the Roses were blowing![2]

Scholars may have recognized that this was not translation, but he
only laughed along with the pedants, since as we have noted, where it
was pointed out to him that his translations from Hafiz were

remarkably personal, Mangan only joked about them being half-his.[3]

Many of the poems "translated" from the German, particularly from minor poets such as Rückert, were about as original as the Oriental ones. Perhaps the most blatant attribution of his own work to a foreign poet was "Twenty Golden Years Ago," whose author, Mangan said, was Selber. As we have seen, Selber did not exist, and his name was only a German derivative for self, or Mangan. Yet Mangan's wry humor could not desist until he had argued the untranslatableness of Selber: "Nobody can translate Selber to advantage. His peculiar idiosyncrasy unfortunately betrays itself in every line he writes, and there exists, moreover, an evident wish on his part to show the world that he possesses 'a life within himself.' "[4] There is more than a little irony in that.

Finally, a last example of Mangan's using his own work and calling it a translation almost breaks the bounds of propriety; but Mangan's indigence could be used to excuse a multitude of sins. In 1832, when Catherine Hayes, a young student of Mangan's, died, her passing produced the poignant "Elegiac Verses on the Death of a Beloved Friend":

> I stood aloof; I dared not to behold
> Thy relics covered over with the mould;
> I shed no tear — I uttered not a groan —
> But yet I felt heartbroken and alone.[5]

In 1838, Mangan published this poem in the *Dublin University Magazine* as a translation from the Irish. Like this poem, Mangan's other translations were, for the most part, nothing of the sort. Translation was for a young writer a means of publication and for a more established writer a catering to the Romantic sensibility of the age.

II *Oriental Translations*

One of Mangan's finer Oriental works is a poem called "The Karamanian Exile" which Mangan called a translation from the Ottoman and published in the *Dublin University Magazine* in 1844. It is a good poem to glance at first because it is stamped with the characteristics which are Mangan's forte. The poem is a lament from an exile who, taken from Karaman while still young, is kept in Ukhbar and has lost his innocence, which he associates with

Karaman. So his bondage is spiritual as well as physical. But Azreel, the Angel of Death, avenges every wrong; and now the exile writes as Ukhbar is about to fall and his hope of freedom is imminent:

> I see thee ever in my dreams,
>> Karaman!
> Thy hundred hills, thy thousand streams,
>> Karaman! O Karaman!
> As when thy gold-bright morning gleams,
> As when the deepening sunset seams
> With lines of light thy hills and streams,
>> Karaman!
> So thou loomest on my dreams,
>> Karaman! O Karaman!
>
> The hot bright plains, the sun, the skies,
>> Karaman!
> Seem death-black marble to mine eyes,
>> Karaman! O Karaman!
> I turn from summer's blooms and dyes;
> Yet in my dreams thou dost arise
> In welcome glory to my eyes,
>> Karaman!
> In thee my life of life yet lies,
>> Karaman!
> Thou still art holy in mine eyes,
>> Karaman! O Karaman!
>
> Ere my fighting years were come,
>> Karaman!
> Troops were few in Erzerome,
>> Karaman! O Karaman!
> Their fiercest came from Erzerome,
> They came from Ukhbar's palace dome,
> They dragged me forth from thee, my home,
>> Karaman!
> Thee, my own, my mountain home,
>> Karaman!
> In life and death, my spirit's home,
>> Karaman! O Karaman!
>
> O, none of all my sisters ten,
>> Karaman!
> Loved like me my fellowmen,

Karaman! O Karaman!
I was mild as milk till then,
I was soft as silk till then;
Now my breast is as a den,
          Karaman!
Foul with blood and bones of men,
          Karaman!
With blood and bones of slaughtered men,
          Karaman! O Karaman!

My boyhood's feelings newly born,
          Karaman!
Withered like young flowers uptorn,
          Karaman! O Karaman!
And in their stead sprang weed and thorn;
What once I loved now moves my scorn;
My burning eyes are dried to horn,
          Karaman!
I hate the blessed light of morn,
          Karaman!
It maddens me, the face of morn,
          Karaman! O Karaman!

The Spahi wears a tyrant's chains,
          Karaman!
But bondage worse than this remains,
          Karaman! O Karaman!
His heart is black with million stains;
Thereon, as on Kaf's blasted plains,
Shall never more fall dews and rains
          Karaman!
Save poison-dews and bloody rains,
          Karaman! O Karaman!
Hell's poison dews and bloody rains,
          Karaman! O Karaman!

But life at worst must end ere long,
          Karaman!
Azreel avengeth every wrong,
          Karaman! O Karaman!
Of late my thoughts rove more among
Thy fields; o'ershadowing fancies throng
My mind, and texts of bodeful song,
          Karaman!
Azreel is terrible and strong,
          Karaman!

> His lightning sword smites all ere long,
>   Karaman! O Karaman!
>
> There's care to-night in Ukhbar's halls,
>   Karaman!
> There's hope too, for his trodden thralls,
>   Karaman! O Karaman!
> What lights flash red along yon walls?
> Hark! hark! — the muster-trumpet calls! —
> I see the sheen of spears and shawls,
>   Karaman!
> The foe! the foe! — they scale the walls,
>   Karaman!
> To-night Muràd or Ukhbar falls,
>   Karaman! O Karaman!
>   (177-179)

Those who argue Mangan's influence upon Poe point to the priority of this poem (published in 1844), among others, to "The Raven" (1845), "Ulalame" (1847), "Lenore," and the like. We may easily see in the poem what calls Poe to mind: Mangan is, like his American contemporary, a master of refrain and haunting melody. In lines such as these we find the alliteration and the internal rhyme so often found in Mangan and in Poe, but we also find that Mangan is using Karaman as an equivalent for Ireland. Colum has pointed out that Mangan constantly attempts an impression of an Irish landscape in a poem and succeeds only in giving lands that are all waste with an isolated tower. Mangan may, as Colum suggests, have been able to look upon his native land only as a country to which foreigners had laid waste.[6]

"The Karamanian Exile" preserves the same ten-line stanza, the same meter, and the same basic rhyme scheme throughout, though the *ababaaabab* rhyme scheme of stanza one becomes, by a change in the rhyming vowel, *cbcbcccbcb* in stanza two, *dbdbdddbdb* in stanza three and so on throughout the eight stanzas. The infectious rhythm of the poem was responsible for James Ryder Randall's "Maryland, My Maryland." Randall, who had been born in Maryland, was moved by the Yankee invasion of Maryland in 1861 to commemorate it by a poem in the *New Orleans Delta*. Before its publication, though, he struggled for a mode of expression; and he tells us that his volume of Mangan had been lying on his desk and that the haunting refrains of "The Karamanian Exile" were running through his mind. After a sleepless night, he settled on the meter of Mangan's poem as just the vehicle for his own.[7]

The same sense of past glory as well as clever use of refrain is to be found in Mangan's oft-anthologized "The Time of the Barmecides." Published in the *Dublin University Magazine* in 1839 and in its final version in 1840, the poem is called a translation from the Arabic. The Barmecides were a famous, noble Persian family which had great power in the eighth century under the Abbasid caliphs; but the family lost favor in the early ninth century and most were put to death. The name itself was the title of their ancestors who were the hereditary high priests of the Buddhist temple. Under their direction, Persia enjoyed a golden period politically and literarily. This period in Bagdad is pictured, however exaggeratedly, in *The Arabian Nights.*

In a poem which is reminiscent, for its theme, of T. S. Eliot's "Sweeney Among the Nightingales," an old man in Mangan's poem harks back to Bagdad's great days — vigorous days "when the angry blow / Supplanted the word that chides" and "when hearts could glow." He knows, however, he is now too old to enjoy such a life; and he relives the time of the Barmecides in memory while waiting for death as a deliverer:

> My eyes are filmed, my beard is grey,
>   I am bowed with the weight of years;
> I would I were stretched in my bed of clay,
>   With my long lost youth's compeers;
> For back to the Past, though the thought brings woe,
>   My memory ever glides —
> To the old, old time, long, long ago,
>   The time of the Barmecides.
>
> Then Youth was mine, and a fierce wild will,
>   And an iron arm in war,
> And a fleet foot high upon Ishkar's hill,
>   When the watch-lights glimmered afar,
> And a barb as fiery as any I know,
>   That Khoord or Beddaween rides,
> Ere my friends lay low — long, long ago,
>   In the time of the Barmecides;
> Ere my friends lay low — long, long ago,
>   In the time of the Barmecides.
>
> One golden goblet illumed my board
>   One silver dish was there;
> At hand my tried Karamanian sword,
>   Lay always bright and bare;
> For those were the days when the angry blow
>   Supplanted the word that chides —

When hearts could glow — long, long ago,
    In the time of the Barmecides;
When hearts could glow — long, long ago
    In the time of the Barmecides.

Through city and desert my mates and I
    Were free to rove and roam,
Our diapered canopy the deep of the sky,
    Or the roof of the palace dome —
O! ours was that vivid life to and fro
    Which only sloth derides —
Men spent Life so, long, long ago,
    In the time of the Barmecides
Men spent Life so, long, long ago,
    In the time of the Barmecides.

I see rich Bagdad once again,
    With its turrets of Moorish mould,
And the Khalif's twice five hundred men,
    Whose binishes flamed with gold;
I call up many a gorgeous show —
    Which the Pall of Oblivion hides —
All passed like snow, long, long ago,
    With the time of the Barmecides;
All passed like snow long, long ago,
    With the time of the Barmecides!

But mine eye is dim, and my beard is grey,
    And I bend with the weight of years —
May I soon go down to the House of Clay
    Where slumber my Youth's compeers!
For with them and the Past, though the thought
    wakes woe,
    My memory ever abides;
And I mourn for the Times gone long ago,
    For the Times of the Barmecides!
I mourn for the Times gone long ago,
    For the Times of the Barmecides!

        (175-176)

Mangan again uses in this poem a mythic golden past to visualize a supposedly similar golden past of Ireland's. And in the realm of the impassioned lament there are few who are Mangan's equal. When he can sing with a Wordsworthian or Byronian sense of past glory, be it national or personal, he is at his best. The refrain, of course, is Mangan's shibboleth, especially the refrain which is never quite repetition; and this relatively new use of an old device gives much of the poignance to his songs. Yet there are other factors, the alliteration and lengthening of vowels, "With its turrets of Moorish mould." And Mangan's haunting rhythm depends too upon a meter which avoids repetition and which uses a felicitous mixture of anapests and iambs:

> Ĭ sée rĭch Bágdăd oňce ağaĭn
>   Wĭth ĭts tŭrrĕts ŏf Móorĭsh móuld,
> Ănd thĕ Cálĭfs̆ tẘice fíve húndrĕd m̆en
>   Whŏse bíniśhĕs flámed wĭth góld.
>   (176)

Yet, though the accents are the same, the same meter is not repeated in the first four lines of the following stanza:

> Bŭt miňe eẙe ĭs̆ dĭm̆ ănd m̆y beárd ĭs̆ grey
>   Ănd Ĭ bénd wĭth thĕ weíght ŏf yeárs
> Măy Ĭ sóon gŏ dówn tŏ thĕ hóuse ŏf cláy
>   Wh̆ere slúmbĕr m̆y yoúth's cŏmpeérs.
>   (176)

Another effective Oriental poem with which the reader of Mangan should be familiar is "The Time of the Roses," which appeared in the *Dublin University Magazine* in May, 1837, and is thematically akin to Keats's great "Ode to Melancholy" or to the later works of A. E. Housman and Edward FitzGerald. The lyric offers a spring scene in which the poet finds implicit the transience of the beauty he sees. He is taught "morality" by this thought, as well as the need to enjoy the fleeting moment of the "time of the roses." Then he wishes he could imprison some of the ephemeral beauties of earth, one of which is the peace that ensues when war is over. And the poet ends by naming himself Meseehi and his love Leila and by contending that she too is a ruse, and that he who seeks repose in her love will least be aware how ephemeral, how passing, is the "time of the roses":

> Morning is blushing; the gay nightingales
> Warble their exquisite song in the vales;
> Spring, like a spirit, floats everywhere,
> Shaking sweet spice-showers loose from her hair,
> Murmurs half-musical sounds from the stream,
> Breathes in the valley and shines in the beam.

In, in at the portals that Youth uncloses,
It hastes, it wastes, the Time of the Roses!

Meadows, and gardens, and sun-lighted glades,
Palaces, terraces, grottoes, and shades
Woo thee; a fairy-bird sings in thine ear,
Come and be happy! — an Eden is here!
Knowest thou whether for thee there be any
Years in the Future? Ah! think on how many
    A young heart under the mould reposes,
    Nor feels how wheels the Time of the Roses!

In the red light of the many-leaved rose,
Mahomet's wonderful mantle re-glows,
Gaudier far, but as blooming and tender,
Tulips and martagons revel in splendour.
Drink from the Chalice of Joy, ye who may!
Youth is a flower of early decay,
    And Pleasure a monarch that Age deposes,
    When past, at last, the Time of the Roses!

See the young lilies, their scymitar petals
Glancing like silver 'mid earthier metals:
Dews of the brightest in life-giving showers
Fall all the night on these luminous flowers,
Each of them sparkles afar like a gem;
Wouldst thou be smiling and happy like them?
    O, follow all counsel that Pleasure proposes;
    It dies, it flies, the Time of the Roses!

Pity the roses! Each rose is a maiden,
Prankt, and with jewels of dew overladen:
Pity the maidens! The moon of their bloom
Rises, to set in the cells of the tomb.
Life has its Winter: — When Summer is gone,
Maidens, like roses, lie stricken and wan;
    Though bright as the Burning Bush of Moses,
    Soon fades, fair maids, the Time of your Roses!

Lustre and odours and blossoms and flowers
All that is richest in gardens and bowers,
Teach us morality, speak of Mortality,
Whisper that Life is a swift Unreality!
Death is the end of that lustre, those odours;

Brilliance and Beauty are gloomy foreboders
    To him who knows what this world of woes is,
    And sees how flees the Time of the Roses!

Heed them not, hear them not! Morning is blushing
Perfumes are wandering, fountains are gushing;
What though the rose, like a virgin forbidden,
Long under leafy pavilion lay hidden;
Now far around as the vision can stretch,
Wreaths for the pencils of angels to sketch,
    Festoon the tall hills the landscape discloses.
    O! Sweet, though fleet, is the Time of the Roses!

Now the air — drunk from the breath of the flowers —
Faints like a bride whom her bliss overpowers;
Such and so rich is the fragrance that fills
Aether and cloud that its essence distils,
As through thin lily-leaves, earthward again,
Sprinkling with rose-water garden and plain,
    O! joyously after the Winter closes,
    Returns and burns the Time of the Roses!

O! for some magical vase to imprison
All the sweet incense that yet has not risen!
And the swift pearls that, radiant and rare,
Glisten and drop through the hollows of Air!
Vain! they depart, both the Beaming and Fragrant!
So, too, Hope leaves us, and Love proves a vagrant,
    Too soon their entrancing illusion closes,
    It cheats, it fleets, the Time of the Roses!

Tempest and Thunder, and War were abroad;
Riot and Turbulence triumphed unawed;
Soliman rose, and the thunders were hushed,
Faction was prostrate, and Turbulence crushed;
Once again Peace in her gloriousness rallies;
Once again shine the glad skies on our valleys;
    And sweetly anew the poet composes
    His lays in praise of the Time of the Roses!

I, too, MESEEHI, already renowned,
Centuries hence by my songs shall be crowned;
Far as the stars of the wide Heaven shine,
Men shall rejoice in this carol of mine.
Leila! Thou art as a rose unto me:

> Think on the nightingale singing for thee;
>   For he who on love like thine reposes,
>   Least heeds how speeds the Time of the Roses!
>   (180-83)

The dactyls again show Mangan's virtuosity and unwillingness to remain with the more straightforward iamb, but the refrain, or the incremental repetition, again is responsible for much of the poignance of the poem.

The structure of the poem too is excellent. It builds through ten stanzas of Keatsian nightingales and Shelleyan gardens bespeaking nature's cycle of birth, death, rebirth, and the need to grasp life while it is there. In the final two stanzas, the poet first introduces the jarring element of war, but it is a war which brings peace. And the poet's wish to seize and contain this peace and "All the sweet incense that yet has not risen" is recognized as futile by the very mention of war and by the reader's awareness of its place in the cycle of nature. And finally the last temptation, to find some permanence in the love of the woman to whom he sings, is seen for what it is: "For he who on love like thine reposes/Least heeds how speeds the Time of the Roses."

The following year, 1838, Mangan published in the *Dublin University Magazine* a fine little verse attributed to the Ottoman, "Lamii's Apology for His Nonsense":

> I was a parrot mute and happy, till
>   Once on a time,
> The fowlers pierced the wood and caught me.
> Then blame me not; for I but echo still
>   In wayward rhyme
> The melancholy wit they taught me.
>   (226)

The basic metaphor of the captive parrot is an effective one; and, like Mangan's Oriental landscape, the bird is obviously and eminently applicable to Ireland's plight. But Mangan is never merely a patriotic poet either. Like Yeats, he transcends narrow nationalism. The Orient can be Ireland, but Ireland can be any place, any suffering place.

Another, slightly longer, translation from the Ottoman, "Sayings of Djelim," had appeared the year before in the *Dublin University*

Magazine; and it is interesting because of its metrics, rhythm, and rhyme, as well as its thought. A fourteen-line poem, it contains quatrains of alternating *abab, dede, fgfg;* but, interestingly, a couplet *cc* is sandwiched in between the first two quatrains. The line is an eight-beat line with chiasma midway, "When Folly sells thee Wisdom's crown, tis idly gained and dearly bought." The internal rhyme, characteristic of Mangan, "Folly," "thee," "idly," "dearly," is seen throughout the poem. And the thought, whether Mangan got it directly from the Ottoman, or more likely from his German readings, seems characteristically that of an Eastern moralist:

> Be circumspect; be watchmanlike; put pebbles in thy mouth each day;
> Pause long ere thou panegyrise; pause doubly long ere thou condemn.
> Thy thoughts are Tartars, vagabonds; imprison all thou canst not slay,
> Of many million drops of rain perchance but one turns out a gem.
>
> (229)

In 1840, Mangan published in the *Dublin University Magazine* a "translation" from the Arabic called "The Howling Song of Al Mohara." Of it Padraic Colum observes, it "might have been made by a magician who had come out of his cell to seize upon words and poetic forms and make of them things to astonish us."[3]

> My heart is as a House of Groans
>   From dusky eve to dawning grey:
>   Allah, Allah hu!
> The glazed flesh on my staring bones
>   Grows black and blacker with decay;
>   Allah, Allah hu!
> Yet am I none whom Death may slay;
> I am spared to suffer and to warn;
>   Allah, Allah hu!
> My lashless eyes are parched to horn
>   With weeping for my sin alway;
>   Allah, Allah hu!
> For blood, hot blood that no man sees,
>   The blood of one I slew
> Burns on my hands I cry therefore,
> All night long, on my knees,
>   Evermore,
>   Allah, Allah hu!
>
> Because I slew him over wine,
>   Because I struck him down at night,

Allah, Allah hu!
Because he died and made no sign,
His blood is always in my sight;
Allah, Allah hu!
Because I raised my arm to smite
While the foul cup was at his lips,
Allah, Allah hu!
Because *I* wrought *his* soul's eclipse
He comes between me and the Light;
Allah, Allah hu!
His is the form my terror sees,
The sinner that I slew;
My rending cry is still therefore,
All night long, on my knees,
Evermore,
Allah, Allah hu!

Under the all-just Heaven's expanse
There is for me no resting-spot;
Allah, Allah hu!
I dread Man's vengeful countenance,
The smiles of Woman win me not;
Allah, Allah hu!
I wander among graves where rot
The carcases of leprous men;
Allah, Allah hu!
I house me in the dragon's den
Till evening darkens grove and grot;
Allah, Allah hu!
But bootless all! — Who penance drees
Must dree it his life through;
My heartwrung cry is still therefore,
All night long, on my knees,
Evermore,
Allah, Allah hu!

The silks that swathe my hall deewan
Are damascened with moons of gold;
Allah, Allah hu!
Musk-roses from my Gulistan
Fill vases of Egyptian mould,
Allah, Allah hu!
The Koran's treasures lie unrolled
Near where my radiant night-lamp burns;
Allah, Allah hu!

Around me rows of silver urns
  Perfume the air with odours old;
      Allah, Allah hu!
    But what avail these luxuries?
    The blood of him I slew
    Burns red on all — I cry therefore,
  All night long on my knees,
      Evermore,
      Allah, Allah hu!

Can Sultans, can the Guilty Rich
  Purchase with mines and thrones a draught,
      Allah, Allah hu!
From that Nutulian fount of which
  The Conscience-tortured whilome quaffed?
      Allah, Allah hu!
  Vain dream! Power, Glory, Riches, Craft,
Prove magnets for the Sword of Wrath;
      Allah, Allah hu!
Thornplant Man's last and lampless path,
  And barb the Slaying Angel's shaft;
      Allah, Allah hu!
    O! the Bloodguilty ever sees
    But sights that make him rue,
    As I do now, and cry therefore,
  All night long, on my knees,
      Evermore,
      Allah, Allah hu!
          (185-88)

The poem reminds the reader of Poe, not only because of its music and subject matter but also because of its constant refrain, "Evermore." And, of course, it was written five years before "The Raven" and helps to bolster the thesis of those who argue Mangan's influence on the American genius of rhythm.

In 1844, the *Dublin University Magazine* published another of Mangan's "translations from the Ottoman," the fine work "The Wail and Warning of the Three Khalendeers." The poem is a nostalgic glance back by one of these three Khalendeers, or wandering dervishes, to times spent boating down the Bosphorus. They were halcyon days, without suffering or materialistic pursuits. And, as the persona talks of these days of happy camaraderie, he leads to the present changed state:

> La' laha, il Allah!
> Ah! for youth's delirious hours
>   Man pays well in after days,
> When quenched hopes and palsied powers
>   Mock his love-and-laughter days;
> Thorns and thistles on our path
>   Took the place of moss for us,
> Till false fortune's tempest wrath
>   Drove us from the Bosphorus!
>   La' laha, il Allah!
>   The Bosphorus, the Bosphorus!
> When thorns took place of moss for us,
> Gone was all! Our hearts were graves
>   Deep, deeper than the Bosphorus!
>   (190)

The Khalendeers have been paid 'for this carefree youth with quenched hopes and aged powers, and now they wail over their lack of foresight:

> La' laha, il Allah!
> Gone is all! In one abyss
>   Lie Health, Youth, and Merriment!
> All we've learned amounts to this —
>   *Life's a sad experiment;*
> What it is we trebly feel
>   Pondering what it was for us,
> When our shallop's bounding keel
>   Clove the joyous Bosphorus!
>   La' laha, il Allah!
>   The Bosphorus, the Bosphorus!
> Youth's fire soon wanes to Phosphorus,
> And slight luck or grace attends
>   Your boaters down the Bosphorus!
>   (190-91)

The poem concludes with "The Warning" in which these "lures hung out by Lucifer" consume man's fire "and bad luck attends and ends/Boatings down the Bosphorus." The seven stanzas of this poem all have the same form, and each begins and ends with the haunting cry "La' laha, il Allah," which Mangan tells us means "God alone is all merciful." And the constant Manganesque refrain about days upon the Bosphorus characteristically builds with incremental repetition so that "Boating down the Bosphorus" becomes by the fifth stanza "Drove us from the Bosphorus."

A very similar poem appeared in the *Dublin University Magazine* in 1845, "The Last Words of Al-Hassan." Mangan, in writing one of his German articles, included the poem as a translation from Von Heyden. However, when O'Donoghue was unable to find it in Von Heyden's poetry, he included it appropriately among Mangan's "Oriental Versions and Perversions." The poem is like the previous one in form, with its repetitious but slightly changing refrain which is so effective:

> My race is run — I am called away —
> I go to the Lampless Land.
> 'Llah Hu!
> I am called away from the light of day
> To my tent in the Dark, Dark Land!
> (200)

However, unlike "The Wailing Song," it does not hark back to any halcyon period. The persona is resigned to death because he has seen too much injustice and unfaithfulness; and, with his friends dead, there is little left for him in this base world. Even his love has disenchanted him:

> Even she, my loved and lost Ameen,
> The moon-white pearl of my soul,
> Could pawn her peace for the show and sheen
> Of silken Istambol!
> How little did I bode what a year would see,
> When we parted at Samarkhand —
> My bride in the harem of the Osmanlee,
> Myself in the Lampless Land!
> 'Llah Hu!
> My bride in the harem of the Osmanlee,
> Myself in the Dark, Dark Land!
> (201)

Yet, in a way reminiscent of the ambivalence found in Yeats's "The Stolen Child," Al-Hassan adverts momentarily to the simple pleasures of nature that he will miss as he turns to the Lampless Land:

> The wasted moon has a marvellous look
>   Amiddle of the starry hordes —
> The heavens, too, shine like a mystic book,
>   All bright with burning words,
> The mists of the dawn begin to dislimn
>   Zahara's castles of sand.
> Farewell — farewell! Mine eyes feel dim —
>   They turn to the Lampless Land.
>   'Llah Hu!
> My heart is weary — mine eyes are dim —
>   I would rest in the Dark, Dark Land!
>   (202)

The internal rhyme and alliteration are once again evident; but, as always, Mangan's use of refrain and incremental repetition lends the greatest power to the work.

The year 1845 was also the one that McGlashan of the *Dublin University Magazine* began to pay Mangan in very small sums lest he consume all his salary on alcohol and opium. Mangan did not appreciate the well-intentioned paternalism, and in 1846 he began to contribute much of his work to *The Nation*. Nevertheless, his Oriental work remained with the *Dublin University Magazine,* and in 1846 he contributed to that magazine a fine poem entitled "Advice":

> Traverse not the globe for lore! The sternest
>   But surest teacher is the heart.
> Studying that and that alone, thou learnest
>   Best and soonest whence and what thou *art*.
>
> *Time* not travel, 'tis which gives us ready
>   Speech, experience, prudence, tact, and wit
> Far more light the lamp that bideth steady
>   Than the wandering lantern doth *emit*.
>
> *Moor;* Chinese, Egyptian, Russian, Roman
>   Tread one common downhill path of doom:
> Everywhere the names are Man and Woman,
>   Everywhere the old sad sins find *room*.
>
> *Evil* angels tempt us in all places.
>   What but sands or snows hath Earth to give?
> Dream not, friend, of deserts and oases,
>   But look inwards, and begin to *live*.
>   (209-10)

This didactic poem in ballad stanzas is listed as a translation from the Ottoman. Nevertheless, it displays another aspect of Mangan's love of word play. We note that, after the opening, the first and last word of each stanza is italicized to point to the fact that the last word is the first word spelled backwards. And even in the first stanza "art" is the first syllable of "Traverse." That "time" should evolve by stanza's end into "emit," "Moor" into "room," and "evil" into "live" is not, of course, just an exercise; but the device gives a circular motion to the work which emphasizes the theme. Geographical travel will not bring wisdom; psychological or spiritual travel will; and such travel will be introspective, will always bring us back to ourselves.

The following year Mangan returned to the *Dublin University Magazine* for the publication of most of his work, including the Irish works like "St. Patrick's Hymn Before Tara." A "translation" appeared in it called "The Worst Loss," a kind of eight-line ballad in which the persona describes through five stanzas various afflictions he has suffered and receives and accepts consolations for the first four troubles before his final loss. In the first stanza, he tells a merchant he has lost the beautiful shawl that the merchant sold him today; and the merchant agrees to make a similar shawl which will not inconvenience such a rich man. Likewise, an architect agrees to rebuild his house that has burnt down. When the speaker drops his money into the river, a boatman consoles him by telling him that he has lost rubbish and that Health and Hope are left him. Even the death of his son is accepted with resignation when the hakim (doctor) assures him: "This youth departs to another Father." But, when he tells Moolah of his last loss, there is no consolation possible:

> "Moolah! Moolah! I feel broken-hearted."
>   — "And why so, son? Whence this bitter anguish?"
>   — "All is gone! My last stay hath departed,
> I *have lost my* NAME!" — "Oh, wretched mortal!
>   Lost thy name! Then, henceforth must thou languish
> In lone woe, shut out from Hope's last portal!
> Go, and consecrate thy soul to God by Sorrow,
> For on thy Life's Night shall never dawn a Morrow!"
>   (193)

Finally, in 1848, the last full year of Mangan's life, after having left St. Vincent's Hospital, Mangan published in the *Dublin University Magazine* a "Turkish" poem somewhat similar in title to an earlier Turkish poem that has been considered. This poem, "The Time Ere the Roses Were Blowing," is, in fact, purported to be a response to the author of "The Time of the Roses"; and it asks that the poet not be so lost in the melancholic fading of the roses that he cannot recall the happy time prior to it:

I

Brilliantly sparkle, Meseehi, thy flowing
Numbers, like streams amid lilies upgrowing,
Yet, wouldst thou mingle the sad and sublime,
    Sing, too, the Time,
Sing the young Time *ere* the Roses were blowing!

II

Then was the Season when Hope was yet glowing
Then the blithe year of the Spring and the Sowing;
Then the Soul dwelt in her own fairy clime;
    Then was the Time,
Then the gay Time *ere* the Roses were blowing!
                (183)

The author then admits that autumn came too soon but life is at best a coming and going. He has a true Oriental acknowledgment of the need for contraries, and he asks Meseehi not to be so one-sided:

V

Coldly, O coldly, goes Truth overthrowing
Fancy's bright palaces, coldly goes mowing
Down the sweet blossoms of Boyhood's young prime.
    Give us the Time,
Give us the Time *ere* the Roses were blowing!

VI

I am Zerba'yeh, the Least of the Knowing;
Thou art Meseehi, the Golden and Glowing!
O, when again thou wouldst dazzle in rhyme

> Sing of the Time,
> Sing of the Time *ere* the Roses were blowing!
> (184)

Whether Mangan "translates" Irish, Turkish, Persian, or German, the ubiquitous refrain lends distinctive music to all his work.

III *German "Translations"*

As we have noted, Mangan was reasonably familiar with German, but one of his finest German "translations" was clearly his own creation, "Selber's" poem "Twenty Golden Years Ago," which appeared in the *Dublin University Magazine* of 1840. The poem is like some of the Oriental poems in that he presents the persona as harking back to better days. As he sits with coffee and gazes out the window at the rain, he thinks of his past glories as a *bon vivant, lothario,* and poet. Now he is left alone, without wife or friends; and he faces death as a curious climax to a life that had once promised so much more than it has realized. Twenty years after his prime, he is a sentimental Rousseauist rather than the grand Byronian he once was:

> O, the rain, the weary, dreary rain,
>   How it plashes on the window-sill!
> Night, I guess too, must be on the wane,
>   Strass and Gass around are grown so still.
> Here I sit, with coffee in my cup —
>   Ah! 'twas rarely I beheld it flow
> In the taverns where I loved to sup
>   Twenty golden years ago!
>
> Twenty years ago, alas! — but stay,
>   On my life, 'tis half-past twelve o'clock!
> After all, the hours *do* slip away —
>   Come, here goes to burn another block!
> For the night, or morn, is wet and cold,
>   And my fire is dwindling rather low: —
> I had fire enough, when young and bold,
>   Twenty golden years ago!
>
> Dear! I don't feel well at all, somehow:
>   Few in Weimar dream how bad I am;
> Floods of tears grow common with me now,
>   High-Dutch floods, that Reason cannot dam.
> Doctors think I'll neither live nor thrive

If I mope at home so — I don't know —
Am I living *now?* I *was* alive
　　Twenty golden years ago.

Wifeless, friendless, flagonless, alone,
　　Not quite bookless, though, unless I chuse
Left with nought to do, except to groan,
　　Not a soul to woo, except the Muse —
O! this, this is hard for *me* to bear,
　　Me, who whilome lived so much *en haut,*
Me, who broke all hearts like chinaware
　　　Twenty golden years ago!

P'rhaps 'tis better: — Time's defacing waves
　　Long have quenched the radiance of my brow —
They who curse me nightly from their graves
　　Scarce could love me were they living now;
But my loneliness hath darker ills —
　　Such dun-duns as Conscience, Thought and Co.,
Awful Gorgons! worse than tailors' bills
　　　Twenty golden years ago!

Did I paint a fifth of what I feel,
　　O, how plaintive you would ween I was!
But I won't, albeit I have a deal
　　More to wail about than Kerner has!
Kerner's tears are wept for withered flowers,
　　Mine for withered hopes; my Scroll of Woe
Dates, alas! from Youth's deserted bowers,
　　　Twenty golden years ago!

Yet may Deutschland's bardlings flourish long!
　　Me, I tweak no beak among them; — hawks
Must not pounce on hawks; besides, in song
　　I could once beat all of them by chalks.
Though you find me, as I near my goal,
　　Sentimentalising like Rousseau,
O! I had a grand Byronian soul
　　Twenty golden years ago!

Tick-tick, tick-tick! — Not a sound save Time's
　　And the windgust, as it drives the rain —
Tortured torturer of reluctant rhymes,
　　Go to bed, and rest thine aching brain!
Sleep! — no more the dupe of hopes or schemes;

> Soon thou sleepest where the thistles blow —
> Curious anticlimax to thy dreams
> Twenty golden years ago!
> (141-43)

Again, we note Mangan's peculiarly effective use of refrain; but the poem also contains another quality that G. K. Chesterton has connected with the older Irish tradition and found lacking in modern Irish poets like Yeats: the faculty of passing easily from the grotesque to the serious literary form and back again. As Chesterton wrote:

Outside Burns you will not find a better instance of verse being common and casual and great than such a verse as this:

> Dear! I don't feel well at all, somehow:
>   Few in Weimar dream how bad I am:
> Floods of tears grow common with me now,
>   High-Dutch floods, that Reason cannot dam.
> Doctors think I'll neither live nor thrive
>   If I mope at home so — I don't know —
> *Am* I living *now?* I *was* alive
>   Twenty golden years ago.

There is something that lingers in such verses as these of Mr. Mangan's, black and bitter and desperate as they are, of an Ireland which is not wholly represented by the later poets; the echoes of an Ireland that fought and feasted and broke hearts and heads in good temper. If it is so, and we have spoiled that gaiety in a people, if we have turned by our continued oppression fighters into mere controversialists and lovers into mere poets, we have a darker charge to answer before God than the bloodiest of the forgotten empires.[9]

More justifiably attributed to the German is one of Mangan's finest poems, "The Ride Round the Parapet." Lady Eleanora von Alleyne is a Strindbergian woman, very alive, very imperious, very scornful of man. She places, as a seemingly insuperable obstacle to the attainment of her hand, a ride around the treacherous parapet of her castle. Knight after knight dies in the attempt to succeed until all knights cease to come. Then, at the height of her hubris, comes Gondibert; and she is captivated by him and sorry she asked him to try the ride around the parapet. When he succeeds, he spurns her; and she is left waiting for a lover until the end of her days when she is transformed into a wooden statue.

Though one of Mangan's longer poems, it is quoted in full:

She said, "I was not born to mope at home in loneliness," —
      The Lady Eleanora von Alleyne.
She said, "I was not born to mope at home in loneliness,
When the heart is throbbing sorest there is balsam in the forest,
        There is balsam in the forest for its pain,"
          Said the Lady Eleanora,
          Said the Lady Eleanora von Alleyne.

She doffed her silks and pearls, and donned instead her hunting-gear,
      The Lady Eleanora von Alleyne.
She doffed her silks and pearls, and donned instead her hunting-gear,
And, till Summer-time was over, as a huntress and a rover,
        Did she couch upon the mountain and the plain,
          She, the Lady Eleanora,
          Noble Lady Eleanora von Alleyne.

Returning home again, she viewed with scorn the tournaments —
      The Lady Eleanora von Alleyne.
Returning home again, she viewed with scorn the tournaments;
She saw the morions cloven and the crowning chaplets woven,
        And the sight awakened only the disdain
          Of the Lady Eleanora,
          Of the Lady Eleanora von Alleyne.

"My feeling towards Man is one of utter scornfulness,"
      Said Lady Eleanora von Alleyne.
"My feeling towards Man is one of utter scornfulness,
And he that would o'ercome it, let him ride around the summit
        Of my battlemented Castle by the Maine,"
          Said the Lady Eleanora,
          Said the Lady Eleanora von Alleyne.

So came a knight anon to ride around the parapet,
      For Lady Eleanora von Alleyne.
So came a knight anon to ride around the parapet,
Man and horse were hurled together o'er the crags that beetled nether —
        Said the Lady, "There, I fancy, they'll remain!"
          Said the Lady Eleanora,
          Queenly Lady Eleanora von Alleyne!

Then came another knight to ride around the parapet,
  For Lady Eleanora von Alleyne.
Then came another knight to ride around the parapet,
Man and horse fell down, asunder, o'er the crags that beetled under —
  Said the Lady, "They'll not leap the leap again!"
   Said the Lady Eleanora,
  Lovely Lady Eleanora von Alleyne!

Came other knights anon to ride around the parapet,
  For Lady Eleanora von Alleyne.
Came other knights anon to ride around the parapet,
Till six-and-thirty corses of both mangled men and horses
  Had been sacrificed as victims at the fane
   Of the Lady Eleanora
  Stately Lady Eleanora von Alleyne!

That woeful year went by, and Ritter none came afterwards
  To Lady Eleanora von Alleyne.
That woeful year was by, and Ritter none came afterwards;
The Castle's lonely basscourt looked a wild o'ergrown-with-grasscourt;
  'Twas abandoned by the Ritters and their train
   To the Lady Eleanora,
  Haughty Lady Eleanora von Alleyne!

She clomb the silent wall, she gazed around her sovran-like,
  The Lady Eleanora von Alleyne!
She clomb the silent wall, she gazed around her sovran-like;
"And wherefore have departed all the Brave, the Lion-hearted,
  Who have left me here to play the Castellain?"
   · Said the Lady Eleanora,
  Said the Lady Eleanora von Alleyne.

"And is it fled for aye, the palmy time of Chivalry?"
  Cried Lady Eleanora von Alleyne.
"And is it fled for aye, the palmy time of Chivalry?
Shame light upon the cravens! May their corses gorge the ravens,
  Since they tremble thus to wear a woman's chain!"
   Said the Lady Eleanora,
  Said the Lady Eleanora von Alleyne.

The story reached at Gratz the gallant Margrave Gondibert
  Of Lady Eleanora von Alleyne.
The story reached at Gratz the gallant Margrave Gondibert.
Quoth he, "I trow the woman must be more or less than human;
  She is worth a little peaceable campaign,

Is the Lady Eleanora,
Is the Lady Eleanora von Alleyne!"

He trained a horse to pace round narrow stones laid merlonwise,
For Lady Eleanora von Alleyne
He trained a horse to pace round narrow stones laid merlonwise —
"Good Grey! do thou thy duty, and this rocky-bosomed beauty
Shall be taught that all the vauntings are in vain
Of the Lady Eleanora,
Of the Lady Eleanora von Alleyne!"

He left his castle halls, he came to Lady Eleanor's,
The Lady Eleanora von Alleyne.
He left his castle-halls, he came to Lady Eleanor's.
"O Lady, best and fairest, here am I, — and, if thou carest,
I will gallop round the parapet amain,
Noble Lady Eleanora,
Noble Lady Eleanora von Alleyne."

She saw him spring to horse, that gallant Margrave Gondibert.
The Lady Eleanora von Alleyne.
She saw him spring to horse, that gallant Margrave Gondibert.
"O, bitter, bitter sorrow! I shall weep for this to-morrow!
It were better that in battle he were slain,"
Said the Lady Eleanora,
Said the Lady Eleanora von Alleyne.

Then rode he round and round the battlemented parapet,
For Lady Eleanora von Alleyne.
Then rode he round and round the battlemented parapet;
The Lady wept and trembled, and her paly face resembled,
As she looked away, a lily wet with rain;
Hapless Lady Eleanora!
Hapless Lady Eleanora von Alleyne!

So rode he round and round the battlemented parapet,
For Lady Eleanora von Alleyne!
So rode he round and round the battlemented parapet;
"Accurst be my ambition! He but rideth to perdition,
He but rideth to perdition without rein!"
Wept the Lady Eleanora,
Wept the Lady Eleanora von Alleyne.

Yet rode he round and round the battlemented parapet,
For Lady Eleanora von Alleyne.

Yet rode he round and round the battlemented parapet.
Meanwhile her terror shook her — yea, her breath well-nigh forsook her,
    Fire was burning in the bosom and the brain
        Of the Lady Eleanora,
    Of the Lady Eleanora von Alleyne!

Then rode he round and off the battlemented parapet
    To Lady Eleanora von Alleyne.
Then rode he round and off the battlemented parapet.
"Now blest be God for ever! This is marvellous! I never
    Cherished hope of laying eyes on thee again!"
        Cried the Lady Eleanora,
    Joyous Lady Eleanora von Alleyne!

"The Man of Men thou art, for thou hast truly conquered me,
    The Lady Eleanora von Alleyne!
The Man of Men thou art, for thou hast fairly conquered me.
I greet thee as my lover, and, ere many days be over,
    Thou shalt wed me and be Lord of my domain,"
        Said the Lady Eleanora,
    Said the Lady Eleanora von Alleyne.

Then bowed the graceful knight, the gallant Margrave Gondibert,
    To Lady Eleanora von Alleyne.
Then bowed that graceful knight, the gallant Margrave Gondibert,
And thus he answered coldly, "There be many who as boldly
    Will adventure an achievement they disdain
        For the Lady Eleanora,
    For the Lady Eleanora von Alleyne.

"Mayest bide until they come, O stately Lady Eleanor!
    O Lady Eleanora von Alleyne!
Mayest bide until they come, O stately Lady Eleanor!
And thou and they may marry, but, for me, I must not tarry;
    I have won a wife already out of Spain,
        Virgin Lady Eleanora,
    Virgin Lady Eleanora von Alleyne.

Thereon he rode away, the gallant Margrave Gondibert.
    From Lady Eleanora von Alleyne.
Thereon he rode away, the gallant Margrave Gondibert.
And long in shame and anguish did that haughty Lady languish,
    Did she languish without pity for her pain
        She the Lady Eleanora,
    She the Lady Eleanora von Alleyne.

And year went after year, and still in barren maidenhood
    Lived Lady Eleanora von Alleyne.
And wrinkled Eld crept on, and still her lot was maidenhood,
And, woe! her end was tragic; she was changed, at length, by magic
    To an ugly wooden image, they maintain;
        She, the Lady Eleanora,
    She, the Lady Eleanora von Alleyne!

And now before the gate, in sight of all, transmogrified,
    Stands Lady Eleanora von Alleyne.
Before her castle gate, in sight of all, transmogrified,
And he that won't salute her must be fined in foaming pewter,
    If a boor — but if a burgher, in champagne,
        For the Lady Eleanora,
    Wooden Lady Eleanora von Alleyne!
            (240-46)

The poem is originally Rückert's, but that author's "Die Begrüssung auf dem Kynast" was a poem inferior to its "translation," as one stanza of Rückert's poem and Mangan's rendering of it make clear:

Sie sprach: Ich will nicht sitzen im stillen Kämmerlein,
    Das Fräulein Künigunde von Kynast!
Ich will zur Jagd ausreiten, zu Rosse sitzt sichs fein,
    Das Fräulein Künigunde!
Sie sprach: Wer mich will freien, der soll ein Ritter sein,
    Das Fräulein Künigunde von Kynast!
Der um dem Kynast reitet, und bricht nicht Hals und Bein.[10]

She said, "I was not born to mope at home in loneliness," —
    The Lady Eleanora von Alleyne.
She said, "I was not born to mope at home in loneliness,
When the heart is throbbing sorest there is balsam in the forest,
    There is balsam in the forest for its pain,"
        Said the Lady Eleanora,
    Said the Lady Eleanora von Alleyne.
            (240-41)

Besides changing Künigunde to Eleanor, it is obvious that Mangan has altered the meter and has changed the ordinary refrain to his favorite, incremental one. He also added internal rhyme to every fourth line, "When the heart is throbbing sorest, there is balsam in the forest." Structurally also Mangan changes the poem, for he doubles its length with twenty-four stanzas of seven lines as opposed to Rückert's twenty-three stanzas, twenty-one of three lines and the first and last of four lines. Mitchel, in telling of how Mangan radically changed Rückert, points out that he kept the final two stanzas because they had the kind of grotesquerie which appealed to his imagination. In the same year and for the same magazine, Mangan created from a Rückert model another poem, "Gone in the Wind." Written in the *ubi sunt* tradition which, as the reader may remember, is a form that goes back to Classical times and was much used by Medieval poets, the poet sometimes begins, sometimes ends his stanzas by asking what has become of great names, persons, places, or things of the past. In doing so, he lends a note of nostalgia and, more important, of the transitory nature of all things of this world. *Ubi sunt* means, of course, "Where are?"; and Dante Rossetti's "Ballad of Dead Ladies," a famous nineteenth-century use of the tradition, ends each stanza with, "Where are the snows of yester-year?" The modern song by Pete Seeger, "Where Have All the Young Flowers Gone?" is a twentieth-century version.

Gone in the Wind

Solomon! where is thy throne? It is gone in the wind.
Babylon! where is thy might? It is gone in the wind.
Like the swift shadows of Noon, like the dreams of the Blind,
Vanish the glories and pomps of the earth in the wind.

Man! canst thou build upon aught in the pride of thy mind?
Wisdom will teach thee that nothing can tarry behind;
Though there be thousand bright actions embalmed and enshrined,
Myriad and millions of brighter are snow in the wind.

Solomon! where is thy throne? It is gone in the wind.
Babylon! where is thy might? It is gone in the wind.
All that the genius of Man hath achieved or designed
Waits but its hour to be dealt with as dust by the wind.

Say, what is Pleasure? A phantom, a mask undefined;
Science? An almond, whereof we can pierce but the rind;

Honour and Affluence? Firmans that Fortune hath signed
Only to glitter and pass on the wings of the wind.

Solomon! where is thy throne? It is gone in the wind.
Babylon! where is thy might? It is gone in the wind.
Who is the Fortunate? He who in anguish hath pined!
He shall rejoice when his relics are dust in the wind!

Mortal! be careful with what thy best hopes are entwined;
Woe to the miners for Truth — where the Lampless have mined!
Woe to the seekers on earth for — what none ever find!
They and their trust shall be scattered like leaves on the wind.

Solomon! where is thy throne? It is gone in the wind.
Babylon! where is thy might? It is gone in the wind.
Happy in death are they only those hearts have consigned
All Earth's affections and longings and cares to the wind.

Pity, thou reader! the madness of poor Humankind,
Raving of Knowledge, — and Satan so busy to blind!
Ráving of Glory, — like me, — for the garlands I bind
(Garlands of song) are but gathered, and — strewn in the wind!

Solomon! where is thy throne? It is gone in the wind.
Babylon! where is thy might? It is gone in the wind.
I, Abul-Namez, must rest; for my fire hath declined,
And I hear voices from Hades like bells on the wind.
                                         (249-50)

Despite its Oriental trappings, the poem seems essentially Christian. All earthly glory, achievement, and pleasure are ephemeral vanities; and the truly fortunate man is not the materially gifted but he "who in anguish hath pined." Furthermore, in a warning like that of Thomas à Kempis's *Imitation of Christ,* we are told that it is not merely materialists who have succumbed to vanity, but those also who in pursuit of knowledge look for it in the wrong places: "Woe to the miners for Truth — where the Lampless have mined!/Woe to the seekers on earth for — what none ever find!"

The metaphors in the fourth stanza are interesting, particularly the comparison of Honour and Affluence to "Firmans." A firman is an edict or permit issued by an Oriental Sovereign. As such, Fortune's signing of these permits "only to glitter and pass on the wings of the wind" is a beautifully apt image for the speaker, Abul-Namez, to use. More interesting than such a metaphor is the experimental rhythm. Mangan uses what might be called dactyllic tetrameter with a final accent on "wind" or its rhyming word in each line:

> Sólomòn! whére is thy thróne? It is góne in the wínd.
> Bábylòn! whére is thy míght? It is góne in the wínd.

The dactyl, of course, gives greater strength to the word opening each line as well as the word beginning each foot. It also suits a poem dealing with the swift passing of pleasures by giving a swifter, more galloping motion than the traditional iamb could. The final accent in each line serves to stress "wind," which is, of course, the crucial word in the poem.

Mangan also uses a rhyme scheme which alternates from stanza to stanza. The first stanza rhymes *aaba* and the second *bbba,* the third *aaba,* the fourth *bbba,* and so on throughout the poem. Also, the odd line in each stanza does have a slant rhyme or approximate rhyme. "Blind" and "wind," for example, are slant rhymes. Although a still greater emphasis remains on "wind," the poet avoids the monotony that would be produced by an *aaaa* rhyme scheme or even by the use of "wind" three times in each stanza.

Finally, the refrain, as in any ballad, lends ritual, form, and emphasis to the poet's theme. The poem is a compelling, incantatory experience; and it demonstrates the irony that Mangan was able to work beautifully from the suggestion of a minor German poet while he usually failed with a major poet. Perhaps, as James Kilroy has suggested in *James Clarence Mangan* (1970), Mangan was intimidated by a Goethe or Schiller; for he seems not to have felt as much at liberty with these poets as he did with Rückert. Moreover, this poem, which appeared in the *Dublin University Magazine* in 1842, indicates that, though Mangan's genius is essentially lyrical, he could excel in the narrative mode. Rückert must have been a kindred spirit for Mangan's best German "translations," or "oversettings," as O'Donoghue calls them, are furnished by Rückert's poems.

A lovely little lyric that appeared in the same magazine three years later reminds us of Byron's "She Walks in Beauty" or perhaps of the life-giving power of the beauty in Shelley's "The Sensitive Plant." In this poem, "And Then No More," the persona sees a woman whose beauty transforms the earth for a time; but the woman vanishes and with her goes the epiphanic aspect of the earth:

> I saw her once, one little while, and then no more:
> 'Twas Eden's light on Earth awhile, and then no more.
> Amid the throng she passed along the meadow-floor:
> Spring seemed to smile on Earth awhile, and then no more;

The poet concludes with the wish that he might terminate his life with the healing power of this vision, this spirit of "intellectual beauty":

> I saw her once, one little while, and then no more:
> The earth was Peri-land awhile, and then no more.
> Oh, might I see but once again, as once before,
> Through chance or wile, that shape awhile, and then no more!
> Death soon would heal my griefs! This heart, now sad and sore,
> Would beat anew a little while, and then no more.
>
> (248-49)

We find in this poem Manganesque hexameter with some internal ryhme, but his feeling for refrain gives the greatest effect to this beautiful lyric.

CHAPTER 3

Irish Poems

MANGAN is best known and most often anthologized for his Irish "translations." These works were at first "translated" by a man who knew no Irish and later by one who knew some of the language. In either case, Mangan added the mark of his own originality, his astonishing rhythms and infectious sounds; and he often changed the original from a meritless work into an effective modern poem.

I *Emergence As National Poet*

Among the Irish poems, the most famous is "Dark Rosaleen," which first appeared in *The Nation* on May 30, 1846; but, though a beautiful poem, it does not deserve to be considered his best. Rosaleen is a personification of Ireland as a maid in distress; yet the poem may originally have been a love poem that was first converted to serve national purposes in Elizabeth's reign.[1] In this poem and others of 1846, Mangan left the light things he had been producing for Duffy in *The Nation* and became political, or at least patriotic, as the national poet of Ireland.

"Dark Rosaleen" was very freely translated from the Irish, for Mangan had come to know some Irish in the previous six years though he was never proficient at it. Although O'Daly and Father Meehan, who was a friend late in Mangan's life, thought he knew no Irish, D. J. O'Donoghue thinks Mangan had acquired by 1846 some knowledge of the language; and most critics agree with O'Donoghue. For this poem, however, he did not need Irish, since he had Ferguson's unrhymed version of the original "Roisin Dubh," which had appeared in the *Dublin University Magazine* in 1834.

"Roisin Dubh," or the Dark-Haired Little Rose, had been written, in the form Mangan used, in Elizabethan times by one of the poets praising the exploits of Hugh Roe O'Donnell or Red Hugh. Hugh is one of two figures, glorified by Irish bards, who play a major role against the English armies during Elizabeth's reign. The other is Hugh O'Neill, a consummate politician who became Lord Dungannon, then Earl of Tyrone, and who plagued the English with whom he was ostensibly allied. Hugh Roe O'Donnell, a much younger warrior, united with O'Neill to achieve some kind of unity against the English. The "cold war" which obtained from 1573 on became a very hot one in the last decade of Elizabeth's reign. Hugh O'Neill was well aware of his military inferiority, but he used tactics designed to delay and harass until perhaps Elizabeth would die, or until Philip of Spain, James VI of Scotland, or the Pope would help. His tactics wore out Essex and his sixteen thousand troops, and Essex agreed to a truce which cost him his head when he returned to England.

However, when Lord Mountjoy came in 1600 with twenty thousand troops and modern equipment, it was a different story. He avoided direct battle, destroyed crops and cattle, and used starvation of the people to bring capitulation. When the Spaniards arrived to help the Irish, the Spanish forces were useless because of their indecisive leader, del Aguila. He entrenched himself in the southern port of Kinsale, was besieged by Mountjoy, and had to have the Northern chiefs hurry to besiege Mountjoy in turn. Dilatory tactics would again have proved successful because Mountjoy was losing confidence, but del Aguila and the youthful Red Hugh O'Donnell persuaded Hugh O'Neill, against his better judgment, to attack. No jointure was effected, the Irish were routed, and in one day the work of ten years was destroyed. O'Donnell fled to Spain and died seeking help; O'Neill capitulated, lived in poverty and humiliation in Tyrone, and fled to Rome when his life was in danger.

In the poem "Dark Rosaleen," Red Hugh O'Donnell addresses his love, Rosaleen. He comforts her in the beginning with the hope of military aid (euphemistically called "wine" or "ale") from the Pope or Spain in an effort to free her from her English captor. He then proceeds to tell how he has struggled for her, been uneasy and concerned over her, prayed for her; and he assures her that he would undertake any task to return her to her rightful throne. The poem ends on a triumphant note which asserts that Rosaleen will perdure until Judgment Day itself. The text of Mangan's poem is reprinted in full:

> O my Dark Rosaleen,
> Do not sigh, do not weep!

The priests are on the ocean green,
   They march along the Deep.
There's wine . . . from the royal Pope
   Upon the ocean green;
And Spanish ale shall give you hope,
   My Dark Rosaleen!
   . . My own Rosaleen!
Shall glad your heart, shall give you hope,
Shall give you health, and help, and hope,
   My Dark Rosaleen.

Over hills and through dales
   Have I roamed for your sake;
All yesterday I sailed with sails
   On river and on lake.
The Erne . . . at its highest flood
   I dashed across unseen,
For there was lightning in my blood,
   My Dark Rosaleen!
   My own Rosaleen!
Oh! there was lightning in my blood,
Red lightning lightened through my blood
   My Dark Rosaleen!

All day long in unrest
   To and fro do I move,
The very soul within my breast
   Is wasted for you, love!
The heart . . . in my bosom faints
   To think of you, my Queen
My life of life, my saint of saints,
   My Dark Rosaleen!
   My own Rosaleen!
To hear your sweet and sad complaints,
My life, my love, my saint of saints,
   My Dark Rosaleen!

Woe and pain, pain and woe
   Are my lot night and noon,
To see your bright face clouded so,
   Like to the mournful moon.
But yet . . . will I rear your throne
   Again in golden sheen;
'Tis you shall reign, shall reign alone,
   My Dark Rosaleen!

My own Rosaleen!
'Tis you shall have the golden throne,
'Tis you shall reign, and reign alone,
   My Dark Rosaleen!

Over dews, over sands
   Will I fly for your weal;
Your holy delicate white hands
   Shall girdle me with steel.
At home . . . in your emerald bowers,
   From morning's dawn till e'en,
You'll pray for me, my flower of flowers,
   My Dark Rosaleen!
   My fond Rosaleen!
You'll think of me through Daylight's hours,
My virgin flower, my flower of flowers,
   My Dark Rosaleen!

I could scale the blue air,
   I could plough the high hills,
Oh, I could kneel all night in prayer,
   To heal your many ills!
And one . . . beamy smile from you
   Would float like light between
My toils and me, my own, my true,
   My Dark Rosaleen!
   My fond Rosaleen!
Would give me life and soul anew,
A second life a soul anew,
   My Dark Rosaleen!

O! the Erne shall run red
   With redundance of blood,
The earth shall rock beneath our tread,
   And flames wrap hill and wood,
And gun-peal, and slogan cry,
   Wake many a glen serene,
Ere you shall fade, ere you shall die,
   My Dark Rosaleen!
   My own Rosaleen!
The Judgment Hour must first be nigh,
Ere you can fade, ere you can die,
   My Dark Rosaleen!
     (3-5)

Padraic Colum is correct in saying that, though the individual stanzas of this poem are finely built, they do not aid the total structure by building idea to idea.[2] Whether this defect is the serious architectural failing he considers it to be is another question since the poem's logic is not tight because it is the cry of an impassioned lover, not of a man arguing a case. As such, the ideas are presented at random; and the only building is toward the final assertion of Rosaleen's permanence in the face of her assailant's continued attack. Colum is correct, however, in praising the structure and exaltation of the individual stanzas:

> Over hílls and thróugh dáles
>   Háve Í róamed for yóur sáke;
> All yésterdáy Í saíled with sáils
>   On river and on lake.
> The Erne . . . at its highest flood
>   I dashed across unseen,
> For there was lightning in my blood,
>   My Dark Rosaleen!
>   My own Rosaleen!
> Oh! there was lightning in my blood,
> Red lightning lightened through my blood,
>   My Dark Rosaleen!
>   (3-4)

The seventh line of this stanza is tremendously moving in context; and the eighth, ninth, and twelfth lines are repeated in each of the seven stanzas but with an occasional, necessary change, "My own Rosaleen" becoming, for example, "My fond Rosaleen." The use of anapest in the stanza's first two lines, which gives way to iambs thereafter, is the interesting pattern followed throughout the poem's stanzas.

The personification of Ireland as the poet's lover comes from the Irish tradition of the *aisling* (vision). Patrick Power describes the formula of the *aisling:* "The poet goes out walking and meets a beautiful lady. He then describes her dress and appearance and asks her who she is. She is generally the personification of Ireland, and she promises early deliverance from the foreign yoke and the return of the Stuarts to the English throne. Sometimes the lady is comforted in this manner by the poet."[3] "Dark Rosaleen" is an adaptation of the form, but it is more rigidly followed by a poem considered below, "The Dream of John McDonnell." Yeats later uses the form to describe Ireland as a personified love, but the universal appeal of

Mangan's poem is not merely derived from its national identification. Mangan's cry is the same more basic one that Blake issues in *America* when he calls for a rebirth of the Orcian principle, the passionate and revolutionary force, to overthrow the Urizenic oppressor, the spirit of abstract, law-making reason so opposed to change. "Rosaleen," therefore, is a poem which asserts hope for the demonic — the inspired quality that exists in every man in the face of the various restraining forces of civilization.

A poem with the same historical context as "Dark Rosaleen" is "Cean Salla," subtitled "The Last Words of Red Hugh O'Donnell on His Departure from Ireland for Spain," which appeared in *The Nation* on July 4, 1846, just five weeks after "Dark Rosaleen." Though not so successful, "Cean Salla" is still an effective short poem:

> Weep not the brave Dead!
>   Weep rather the Living —
>   On them lies the curse
> Of a doom unforgiving!
> Each dark hour that rolls,
>   Shall the memories they nurse,
> Like molten hot lead,
> Burn into their souls
>   A remorse long and sore!
>   They have helped to enthral a
>   Great land evermore,
>   They who fled from Cean-Salla!
>
> Alas, for thee, slayer
>   Of the kings of the Norsemen!
>   Thou land of sharp swords,
> And strong kerns and swift horsemen!
>   Land ringing with song!
>   Land, whose abbots and lords,
>   Whose Heroic and Fair,
>   Through centuries long,
>   Made each palace of thine
>   A new western Walhalla —
> Thus to die without sign
>   On the field of Cean-Salla;
>
> My ship cleaves the wave —
>   I depart for Iberia —
>   But, oh! with what grief,

> With how heavy and dreary a
>   Sensation of ill!
> I should welcome a grave:
>   My career has been brief,
> But I bow to God's will!
> Yet if now all forlorn,
>   In my green years, I fall, a
> Long exile I mourn —
>   But I mourn for Cean-Salla!
>   (48-49)

The rhythm is like that of some of Byron's shorter poems, especially "Fare Thee Well Fanny"; but Mangan's admiration for Byron sometimes served him poorly. The tripping meter is not well suited to the theme, and furthermore, the hudibrastic rhyme, which was Byron's trademark, served the humor of *Don Juan* well but hurts this poem which does not intend to amuse. Byron could ask, "But O ye lords of ladies intellectual/Inform us truly have they not henpecked you all," and attain the humor he intended from the rhyming of one polysyllabic word with a number of monosyllabic words. However, Mangan's rhyming of "Iberia" and "dreary a" or "I fall a" and "Cean-Salla" gives some of the same sense of the ludicrous that hudibrastic rhyme carries without Mangan's intending it to do so.

Another fine poem in which Ireland is personified is "The Dream of John MacDonnell." A work less discussed than some of Mangan's other Irish poems, it is worthy of the author of "Dark Rosaleen." The original was the Irish poem of an eighteenth-century Ulster poet, John MacDonnell, who describes the guardian spirit of Erin as having appeared to him in a dream. Not knowing who the "tall, fair figure" was, whether Banshee or Angel, he begins a search for her when she disappeared. The journey leads to Gruagach's mansion in the North; to Inverlough; to the shining strand of the fishful Erne; above the Boyne's broad waters to Tara, the glory of Erin; and finally to the royal towers of Ival. Here, at last, the mysterious woman reveals herself to him as the Guardian Spirit of Erin. She also reveals to him that her son and heir is in exile in a far land, and the poet wakes to the sorrow of the vision:

> I lay in unrest — old thoughts of pain,
>   That I struggled in vain to smother,
> Like midnight spectres haunted my brain —

   Dark fantasies chased each other;
When, lo! a Figure — who might it be —
   A tall fair figure stood near me!
Who might it be? An unreal Banshee?
     Or an angel sent to cheer me?

Though years have rolled since then, yet now
     My memory thrillingly lingers
On her awful charms, her waxen brow,
     Her pale, translucent fingers,
Her eyes that mirrored a wonder-world,
     Her mien of unearthly mildness,
And her waving raven tresses that curled
     To the ground in beautiful wildness.

"Whence comest thou, Spirit?" I asked, methought;
     "Thou art not one of the Banished!"
Alas, for me! she answered nought,
     But rose aloft and evanished;
And a radiance, like to a glory, beamed
     In the light she left behind her.
Long time I wept, and at last medreamed
     I left my shieling to find her.

And first I turned to the thunderous North,
     To Gruagach's mansion kingly;
Untouching the earth I then sped forth
     To Inver-lough, and the shingly
And shining strand of the fishful Erne,
     And thence to Cruachan the golden,
Of whose resplendent palace ye learn
     So many a marvel olden —

I saw the Mourna's billows flow —
     I passed the walls of Shenady,
And stood in the hero-thronged Ardroe,
     Embosked amid greenwoods shady;
And visited that proud pile that stands
     Above the Boyne's broad waters,
Where Aengus dwells, with his warrior-bands
     And the fairest of Ulster's daughters.

To the halls of MacLir, to Creevroe's height,
     To Tara, the glory of Erin,
To the fairy palace that glances bright

On the peak of the blue Cnocfeerin,
    I vainly hied. I went west and east —
    I travelled seaward and shoreward —
But thus was I greeted at field and at feast —
    "Thy way lies onward and forward!"

At last I reached, I wist not how,
    The royal towers of Ival,
Which under the cliff's gigantic brow,
    Still rise without a rival;
And here were Thomond's chieftains all,
    With armour, and swords, and lances,
And here sweet music filled the hall
    And damsels charmed with dances.

And here, at length, on a silvery throne,
    Half seated, half reclining,
With forehead white as the marble stone,
    And garments so starrily shining,
And features beyond the poet's pen —
    The sweetest, saddest features —
Appeared before me once again,
    The fairest of Living Creatures!

"Draw near, O mortal!" she said with a sigh,
    "And hear my mournful story!
The Guardian-Spirit of Erin am I,
    But dimmed is mine ancient glory;
My priests are banished, my warriors wear
    No longer victory's garland;
And my Child, my Son, my beloved Heir,
    Is an exile in a far land!"

I heard no more — I saw no more —
    The bands of slumber were broken;
And palace and hero, and river and shore,
    Had vanished and left no token.
Dissolved was the spell that had bound my will
    And my fancy thus for a season;
But a sorrow therefore hangs over me still,
    Despite of the teachings of Reason!
                 (6-8)

Historically, the child mentioned in the next-to-last stanza is the
Young Pretender, Prince Charles, grandson of King James II, whom

the Irish wanted to replace the Hanovers. In fact, the poem is an excellent example of the bardic *aisling* or dream-vision discussed in connection with "Dark Rosaleen." This poem lacks the usual refrain one finds in Mangan, and the stanzas are essentially two ballad stanzas joined as one — a Wordsworthian trait. The poem has the ballad simplicity, and its beauty lies in the straightforward way in which the poet's quest for the vanished lady is presented, as his pursuit of the spirit takes him through places which conjure up Ireland's past greatness. "The Dream of John MacDonnell" appeared in *The Nation* on May 16, 1846, and in the same year appeared one of Mangan's truly memorable Irish poems, "O'Hussey's Ode to the Maguire," which was published in H. R. Montgomery's *Specimens of Early, Native Poetry of Ireland* (1846). As in "Dark Rosaleen," Mangan depended upon a translation of the original by Fergusson. O'Hussey was the last bard of the Maguire sept, or clan, and his chief, Hugh, accompanied Hugh O'Neill into the south to confederate chieftains against Queen Elizabeth.

The Irish had not fared well under Elizabeth. She had not begun the "Plantations" policy, but it had become under her a religious phenomenon. Ironically, the Catholic Mary Tudor had initiated the policy of replacing Irish of questionable allegiance to the crown with English whose loyalty was established. With Elizabeth, it became, though for the same reason, the replacing of Catholic with Protestant. Some of these plantations, as in Munster, could be rationalized as acts of war. Others, as in Ulster, were cold-blooded acts in time of peace. Five hundred thousand acres were given to Scottish and English "undertakers" in parcels of one to two thousand acres, and they would then sublet plots to Irish tenants but with no title and revocable at will. Under Elizabeth's plantation policy, roughly one-third of Irish land was taken from the original owners and under later Cromwellian confiscations at least another third. By the time of the penal laws, which followed the Battle of the Boyne in 1690, nine-tenths of Irish land had been taken from its original owners; and no Catholic was allowed to purchase more than two acres of land in the final confiscation, nor to acquire any land by gift from a Protestant. It was, then, to unify the Irish against an oppressor that Maguire made the journey of which the poet sings. He never returned; he died heroically in battle outside Cork when he and the English captain, St. Leger, slew each other.

The poem opens with O'Hussey's asking where his chief is on this cold, sleety night. Then, in a description of the weather which becomes constantly more bleak and violent, the poet remarks that nothing is crueler than the weather this evening except the hatred that persecutes his chieftain. Thus the elements become an evident symbol of the anger and hatred of some of the unpatriotic chieftains which Hugh Maguire experiences "in the country of Clan Darry." Even the animals accustomed to such weather cannot bear it; and the poet continues, "Before him and behind triumphs the tyrannous anger of the wounding wind." Maguire becomes a kind of Lear figure as he continues his lament that "his great hand, so oft the avenger of the oppressed, should . . . be paralyzed by frost." Yet, despite the raging of the elements against him, Hugh is kept warm by the thoughts of his past glories. This memory "a warm dress is to him that lightning-garb he ever wore,/The lightning of the soul, not skies." The poem is quoted in its entirety:

Where is my Chief, my Master, this bleak night, *mavrone!*
O, cold, cold, miserably cold is this bleak night for Hugh,
It's showery, arrowy, speary sleet pierceth one through and through
Pierceth one to the very bone!

Rolls real thunder? Or was that red, livid light
Only a meteor? I scarce know; but through the midnight dim
The pitiless ice-wind streams. Except the hate that persecutes *him*
Nothing hath crueller venomy might.

An awful, a tremendous night is this, meseems!
The flood-gates of the rivers of heaven, I think, have been burst wide —
Down from the overcharged clouds, like unto headlong ocean's tide,
Descends grey rain in roaring streams.

Though he were even a wolf ranging the round green woods,
Though he were even a pleasant salmon in the unchainable sea,
Though he were a wild mountain eagle, he could scarce bear, he,
This sharp, sore sleet, these howling floods.

O, mournful is my soul this night for Hugh Maguire!
Darkly, as in a dream, he strays! Before him and behind
Triumphs the tyrannous anger of the wounding wind,
The wounding wind, that burns as fire!

It is my bitter grief — it cuts me to the heart —
That in the country of Clan Darry this should be his fate!
O, woe is me, where is he? Wandering, houseless, desolate,
Alone, without or guide or chart!

Medreams I see just now his face, the strawberry bright,
Uplifted to the blackened heavens, while the tempestuous winds
Blow fiercely over and round him, and the smiting sleet-shower blinds
The hero of Galang to-night!

Large, large affliction unto me and mine it is,
That one of his majestic bearing, his fair, stately form,
Should thus be tortured and o'erborne — that this unsparing storm
Should wreak its wrath on head like his!

That his great hand, so oft the avenger of the oppressed,
Should this chill, churlish night, perchance, be paralysed by frost —
While through some icicle-hung thicket — as one lorn and lost
He walks and wanders without rest.

The tempest-driven torrent deluges the mead,
It overflows the low banks of the rivulets and ponds —
The lawns and pasture-grounds lie locked in icy bonds
So that the cattle cannot feed.

The pale bright margins of the streams are seen by none.
Rushes and sweeps along the untamable flood on every side —
It penetrates and fills the cottagers' dwellings far and wide —
Water and land are blent in one.

Through some dark woods, 'mid bones of monsters, Hugh now strays,
As he confronts the storm with anguished heart, but manly brow —
O! what a sword-wound to that tender heart of his were now
A backward glance at peaceful days.

But other thoughts are his — thoughts that can still inspire
With joy and an onward-bounding hope the bosom of Mac-Nee —
Thoughts of his warriors charging like bright billows of the sea,
Borne on the wind's wings, flashing fire!

And though frost glaze to-night the clear dew of his eyes,
And white ice-gauntlets glove his noble fine fair fingers o'er,
A warm dress is to him that lightning-garb he ever wore,
The lightning of the soul, not skies.

AVRAN

Hugh marched forth to the fight — I grieved to see him so depart;
And lo! to-night he wanders frozen, rain-drenched, sad, betrayed —
But the memory of the lime-white mansions his right hand hath laid
In ashes warms the hero's heart!

(8-11)

Colum has said that the verse "is like the storm that spends its fury upon the chieftain addressed; it rises and falls, pauses and lashes out."[4] The verse is composed of four-line stanzas rhyming *abba;* the lines are unequal in their length, the fourth line always having four beats but the first three varying between six and seven. This irregularity is also found in the unaccented syllables. Mangan moves from iambs to dactyls or anapests. The verse cannot but remind the reader of Gerard Manley Hopkins's sprung rhythm, and it could have come from that other anticipator of Hopkins, Samuel Taylor Coleridge, who uses a similar freedom in *Christabel.* More probably, however, the verse is taken from the alliterative and rhyming long line used by the *filid,* or ancient Irish poets.

Filid (singular *file* or *fili*), as the pre-thirteenth-century bards were called, seem to have been descendants of the ancient Druids. The pagan priests had been succeeded by the bards about the time of St. Patrick. These poets were also thaumaturges, medicine men; and later they were troubadours, scholars, archivists, and court poets kept by chieftains. Their power among the people was such that the English, who could not destroy them, tried to use them, as when Mountjoy seduced Angus O'Daly to write against the Irish chieftains, something for which O'Daly paid with his life at the hands of his own countrymen.

Bardic schools were to last until the eighteenth century. Young men would come to study under a master, and the people would care for their upkeep. After a topic had been discussed in the morning, the students retired to their cells to meditate and compose in the dark and often with a stone on the chest. Then they wrote their works down, read them in the afternoon, and in the evening everyone gathered for a general criticism. Since poems could be very lengthy series of quatrains, bardic feats of memory were prodigious. The oldest form of verse that the *filid* used was nonrhyming, alliterative verse. Rhyme made its appearance in the seventh century, and there are those who claim that the Celt taught Europe to use it. A later bardic form, destined to become the most popular form, was the *debide.* The *debide* (cut in two) was essentially a quatrain composed of two couplets, generally heptasyllabic or octosyllabic, and regularly containing a very difficult bardic technique, the *aird-rinn.* In this device, the rhyming word of the second line contained a syllable more than that of the first line; likewise, the fourth line's rhyming word contained one more than the third's. Also, if the accent fell on the last syllable in the first line, it usually fell on the next-to-last syllable in the second line. If the accent fell on the penultimate syllable in the first line, it would fall on the antepenult in the second.

O'Hussey wrote in this difficult *debide* form, but Mangan wisely did not try to recapture such a *tour de force*. Rather, he seems to have used the more ancient, long alliterative line, added rhyme, and welded the whole thing into his own pliable medium. With such a free meter, Mangan is able to convey the wild, lashing fury of the elements as they strike this Lear figure and make him feel the coldness and rejection of his fellow chieftains. And, just as the ode verges on the tragic, the fury of the verse subsides because the Maguire has found a source of warmth, of inner strength, amid the oppressiveness of the storm. He has found that "a warm dress is to him that lightning-garb he ever wore,/The lightning of the soul, not skies."

Reading the "Ode to the Maguire" is a truly moving experience, for the poem brings the chief through a kind of final battle to inner victory; and, as Padraic Colum says, through the rush of the verse "comes something of the masculine, extravagant world of the Gaelic bards."[5]

II *Development into National Poet*

Another popular Irish poem dates from the period in which Mangan produced "Twenty Golden Years Ago," 1840 — the elegy, "Lament for the Princes of Tyrone and Tyrconnell (Buried in Rome)." The event concerned has been referred to in our discussion of "Dark Rosaleen." O'Neill remained in Tyrone after the defeat at Kinsale in 1601 to suffer poverty and humiliation, but under the peaceful conditions established by Mountjoy. The next deputy, Chichester, did not respect the peace; and O'Neill fled to Rome in 1607 along with the Earl O'Donnell (Rory, son of Hugh) and one hundred earls of Ulster. The flight seems to have been immediately necessitated by a libelous charge that the Northern earls were plotting to overthrow the government. Their flight preceded that of Patrick Sarsfield and the "Wild Geese" by eighty-one years. Consequently, they represent the first large group of Irish exiles and the first great Irish loss of talent and leadership — an event referred to in Irish history as the "Flight of the Earls." The bodies of O'Neill and the Irish princes are buried in one grave on St. Peter's Hill in Rome; and, as Louise Imogen Guiney indicates, "No Irish pilgrim ascends the Janiculum without thinking of Mangan and mentally repeating 'O Woman of the Piercing Wail.' "

Mangan's elegy follows the form of the regular ode, and the poem is very simple in theme. The Woman of the Piercing Wail, to whom the poem is addressed, is the O'Donnell's sister, who was also an exile. The original Irish poet, Hugh Macward, tells the woman that she would not mourn alone had these princes been fortunate enough to die at home. He lists the famous Irish place-names that would mourn them — Shannon, Boyne, and the Derby plain, among many others in the catalogue. In an interesting transference of the grave itself, he sings that many horses would have trampled down the hill of St. Peter where they lie. Then, after alluding to some of the great who are buried there, the poem continues to the end, remarking the different fate that would be theirs had they died at home on the battlefield. The final three stanzas are a religious resignation to the providence of God and a renunciation of worldly glory in favor of following in Christ's footsteps. But the poet hopes that God in his providence will "render light the chain" that binds his fallen land and watch over Erin's fate.

The conclusion has the ambiguity that naturally springs from a Christian people who are trying to throw off an oppressor. It seems to forswear the glory whose absence the rest of the poem laments, a paradox inherent in the Christian tradition. It combines the Old Testament militancy of the Chosen People with a Pauline resignation to one's lot. The result is not a harmful ambiguity in the poem but one which gives a certain dynamic quality to the poem and renders it more universal. Padraic Colum has called the work Mangan's greatest Irish poem after "O'Hussey's Ode to the Maguire," and he admires the structural power in it which he finds lacking in "Dark Rosaleen":

> O Woman of the Piercing Wail,
>   Who mournest o'er yon mound of clay
>   With sigh and groan,
> Would God thou wert among the Gael!
>   Thou wouldst not then from day to day
>   Weep thus alone.
> 'Twere long before, around a grave
>   In green Tirconnell, one could find
>   This loneliness;
> Near where Beann-Boirche's banners wave
>   Such grief as thine could ne'er have pined
>   Companionless.

Beside the wave, in Donegall,
  In Antrim's glens, or fair Dromore,
    Or Killilee,
Or where the sunny waters fall,
  At Assaroe, near Erna's shore,
    This could not be.
On Derry's plains — in rich Drumclieff —
  Throughout Armagh the Great, renowned
    In olden years,
No day could pass but Woman's grief
  Would rain upon the burial-ground
    Fresh floods of tears!

O, no! — from Shannon, Boyne, and Suir,
  From high Dunluce's castle-walls,
    From Lissadill,
Would flock alike both rich and poor,
  One wail would rise from Cruachan's halls
    To Tara's hill;
And some would come from Barrow-side,
  And many a maid would leave her home
    On Leitrim's plains,
And by Melodious Banna's tide
  And by the Mourne and Erne, to come
    And swell thy strains!

O, horses' hoofs would trample down
  The Mount whereon the martyr-saint
    Was crucified.
From glen and hill, from plain and town,
  One loud lament, one thrilling plaint
    Would echo wide.
There would not soon be found, I ween
  One foot of ground among those bands
    For museful thought,
So many shriekers of the *keen*
  Would cry aloud, and clap their hands,
    All woe-distraught!

Two princes of the line of Conn
  Sleep in their cells of clay beside
    O'Donnell Roe:
Three royal youths, alas! are gone,
  Who lived for Erin's weal, but died

                    For Erin's woe!
Ah! could the men of Ireland read
    The names these noteless burial-stones
        Display to view,
Their wounded hearts afresh would bleed,
    Their tears gush forth again, their groans
        Resound anew!

The youths whose relics moulder here
    Were sprung from Hugh, high Prince and Lord
        Of Aileach's land.
Thy noble brothers, justly dear,
    Thy nephew, long to be deplored
        By Ulster's bands.
Theirs were not souls wherein dull Time
    Could domicile Decay or house
        Decrepitude!
They passed from earth ere Manhood's prime,
    Ere years had power to dim their brows
        Or chill their blood.

And who can marvel o'er thy grief,
    Or who can blame thy flowing tears,
        That knows their source?
O'Donnell, Dunnasava's chief,
    Cut off amid his vernal years,
        Lies here a corse
Beside his brother Cathbar, whom
    Tirconnell of the Helmets mourns
        In deep despair —
For valour, truth, and comely bloom,
    For all that greatens and adorns,
        A peerless pair.

O, had these twain, and he, the third,
    The Lord of Mourne, O'Niall's son,
        Their mate in death —
A prince in look, in deed, and word —
    Had these three heroes yielded on
        The field their breath,
O, had they fallen on Criffan's plain,
    There would not be a town or clan
        From shore to sea
But would with shrieks bewail the Slain
    Or chant aloud the exulting rann
        Of jubilee!

When high the shout of battle rose,
　　On fields where Freedom's torch still burned
　　　　Through Erin's gloom,
If one, if barely one of those
　　Were slain, all Ulster would have mourned
　　　　The hero's doom!
If at Athboy, where hosts of brave
　　Ulidian horsemen sank beneath
　　　　The shock of spears,
Young Hugh O'Neill had found a grave,
　　Long must the North have wept his death
　　　　With heart-wrung tears!

If on the day of Ballach-myre
　　The Lord of Mourne had met, thus young,
　　　　A warrior's fate,
In vain would such as thou desire
　　To mourn, alone, the champion sprung
　　　　From Niall the Great!
No marvel this — for all the Dead,
　　Heaped on the field, pile over pile,
　　　　At Mallach-brack,
Were scarce an eric for his head,
　　If Death had stayed his footsteps while
　　　　On Victory's track!

If on the Day of Hostages
　　The fruit had from the parent bough
　　　　Been rudely torn
In sight of Munster's bands — Mac-Nee's —
　　Such blow the blood of Conn, I trow,
　　　　Could ill have borne.
If on the day of Ballach-boy
　　Some arm had laid, by foul surprise,
　　　　The chieftain low,
Even our victorious shout of joy
　　Would soon give place to rueful cries
　　　　And groans of woe!

If on the day the Saxon host
　　Were forced to fly — a day so great
　　　　For Ashanee
The Chief had been untimely lost,
　　Our conquering troops should moderate
　　　　Their mirthful glee.
There would not lack on Lifford's day

From Galway, from the glens of Boyle,
  From Limerick's towers,
    A marshalled file, a long array
Of mourners to bedew the soil
  With tears in showers!

If on the day a sterner fate
  Compelled his flight from Athenree,
    His blood had flowed,
What numbers all disconsolate
  Would come unasked, and share with thee
    Affliction's load!
If Derry's crimson field had seen
  His life-blood offered up, though 'twere
    On Victory's shrine,
A thousand cries would swell the *keen*
  A thousand voices in despair
    Would echo thine!

Oh, had the fierce Dalcassian swarm
  That bloody night on Fergus' banks,
    But slain our Chief,
When rose his camp in wild alarm —
  How would the triumph of his ranks
    Be dashed with grief!
How would the troops of Murbach mourn
  If on the Curlew Mountains' day,
    Which England rued,
Some Saxon hand had left them lorn,
  By shedding there, amid the fray,
    Their prince's blood!

Red would have been our warriors' eyes
  Had Roderick found on Sligo's field
    A gory grave,
No Northern Chief would soon arise
  So sage to guide, so strong to shield,
    So swift to save.
Long would Leith-Cuinn have wept if Hugh
  Had met the death he oft had dealt
    Among the foe;
But, had our Roderick fallen too,
  All Erin must, alas! have felt
    The deadly blow!

What do I say? Ah, woe is me!
  Already we bewail in vain
      Their fatal fall!
And Erin, once the Great and Free,
    Now vainly mourns her breakless chain,
        And iron thrall!
Then, daughter of O'Donnell! dry
    Thine overflowing eyes, and turn
        Thy heart aside!
For Adam's race is born to die,
    And sternly the sepulchral urn
        Mocks human pride!

Look not, nor sigh for earthly throne,
    Nor place thy trust in arm of clay —
        But on thy knees
Uplift thy soul to God alone,
    For all things go their destined way
        As He decrees.
Embrace the faithful Crucifix,
    And seek the path of pain and prayer
        Thy Saviour trod;
Nor let thy spirit intermix
    With earthly hope and worldly care
        Its groans to God!

And thou, O mighty Lord! whose ways
    Are far above our feeble minds
        To understand,
Sustain us in these doleful days,
    And render light the chain that binds
        Our fallen land!
Look down upon our dreary state,
    And through the ages that may still
        Roll sadly on,
Watch Thou o'er hapless Erin's fate,
    And shield at least from darker ill
        The blood of Conn!
            (17-24)

The poem is in the long tradition of the keen, or *caoine* — the elegy
or lament sung three hours after death at an Irish wake. It can be
passed over by the non-Irish reader more easily than some lesser

poems. However, a second or third reading aloud makes us yield to its imaginative scenes and noble, infectious rhythm. Louise Imogen Guiney has referred to its "intense monotony" which she compares to the Homeric catalogue. However, "intense monotony" is also characteristic of the keen whose purpose is to arouse pity for the deceased and which sometimes resorted to a wordless cry for that end.

In the same year, Mangan wrote another kind of Irish poem, "The Woman of Three Cows." Despite this poem and the previous one, Mangan still knew nothing yet of the Irish language, which he subsequently studied. In fact, "The Woman of Three Cows" may have been the catalyst which began his search into the Irish language, for the poem is taken from the Irish, and it appeared in the *Irish Penny Journal* on August 29, 1840. In it, the poet chides a woman for her overweening pride in her estate; for her three cows enable her to lord it over her inferiors who have just two. To make the woman conscious of her hubris, the poet recalls the great heroes of Ireland who have seen their glory fade. The poem has a whimsical irony which brings out a side of Mangan seen too seldom in his more famous work. The poem is offered in full:

O Woman of Three Cows, agragh! don't let your tongue thus rattle!
O don't be saucy, don't be stiff, because you may have cattle.
I've seen (and here's my hand to you, I only say what's true!)
A many a one with twice your stock not half so proud as you.

Good luck to you, don't scorn the poor, and don't be their despiser,
For worldly wealth soon melts away, and cheats the very miser.
And death soon strips the proudest wreath from haughty human brows:
Then don't be stiff, and don't be proud, good Woman of Three Cows!

See where Momonia's heroes lie, proud Owen More's descendants!
'Tis they that won the glorious name and had the grand attendants!
If they were forced to bow to fate, as every mortal bows,
Can you be proud, can you be stiff, my Woman of Three Cows?

The brave sons of the Lord of Clare, they left the land to mourning.
Mavrone! for they were banished, with no hope of their returning:
Who knows in what abodes of want those youths were driven to house?
Yet you can give yourself these airs, O Woman of Three Cows!

O think of Donnell of the Ships, the chief whom nothing daunted!
See how he fell in distant Spain, unchronicled, unchanted!
He sleeps, the great O'Sullivan, whom thunder cannot rouse:
Then ask yourself, should you be proud, good Woman of Three Cows!

O'Ruark, Maguire, those souls of fire whose names are shrined in story,
Think how their high achievements once made Erin's greatest glory;
Yet now their bones lie mouldering under weeds and cypress boughs,
And so, for all your pride, will yours, O Woman of Three Cows!

The O'Carrolls, also, famed when fame was only for the boldest,
Rest in forgotten sepulchres with Erin's best and oldest;
Yet who so great as they of yore in battle and carouse?
Just think of that, and hide your head, good Woman of Three Cows.

Your neighbour's poor, and you, it seems, are big with vain ideas,
Because, inagh, you've got three cows; one more, I see, than she has!
That tongue of yours wags more, at times, than charity allows:
But if you're strong, be merciful, great Woman of Three Cows!

Summing Up

Now there you go: you still, of course, keep up your scornful bearing;
And I'm too poor to hinder you. But, by the cloak I'm wearing,
If I had but four cows myself, even though you were my spouse,
I'd thwack you well to cure your pride, my Woman of Three Cows!
(13-15)

Mangan's use of hyperbole is excellent. He conjures up a list of great
names in a kind of *ubi sunt* manner to lend a spirit of the mock-
heroic to the poem. The Summing Up even brings to mind the great
Ulster Cycle saga, the *Táin Bó Cúailnge* (Cattle Raid of Cooley), in
which Cuchulain's epic struggle is precipitated after Queen Maeve
and her husband, Ailill, quarrel in bed over a bull and Maeve has to
go to war to acquire a finer bull than her husband's. The long hep-
tameter couplets are well suited to the ironic theme, and the
hudibrastic rhyming of words like "carouse" and "Three Cows" or
"ideas" and "she has" helps the humorous spirit of this fine poem.

Five months after writing "The Woman of Three Cows," Mangan
produced "Kathaleen Ny-Houlahan" for the same *Irish Penny Jour-*
nal. "Ny" is the feminine equivalent of the masculine "O" or
"Mac"; and, as in Yeats's play, Ireland is personified. Kathaleen is

Dark Rosaleen, and the poet insists on her beauty however unapparent it is at the moment: "Were the king's son at home here with Kathaleen Ny-Houlahan/Sweet and mild would look her face." The time of the poem is during the Jacobite rebellions, that of the "Old Pretender" James in 1715 and that of the "Young Pretender" Charles Edward in 1745. And the king's son for whom she waits is the Young Pretender, Charles Edward; but Irish Jacobites were frustrated in their attempt to bring the Stuart prince to the throne. The poem calls upon the God of Israel to "cast a look of pity on Kathaleen Ny-Houlahan"; and, as with other Irish nationalist poems, the struggle takes on a messianic spirit by being connected with the chosen people.

It is difficult to understand what Padraic Colum means by calling this poem the "happiest of Mangan poems"[6] unless he means felicitous in its technique. The poem looks to Kathaleen's deliverance but, like most of the Jacobite poems, without a great deal of optimism. And what hurts Irish sensibilities most is the notion that she is enslaved by the inferior eighteenth-century Hanovers, "Sore disgrace it is to see the Arbitress of thrones/Vassal to a *Saxoneen* of cold and sapless bones" (16). As for the technique, the poem has the characteristic Manganesque trademarks, a refrain which changes slightly and grows with each successive stanza so that "But their hope is in the coming-to of Kathaleen Ny-Houlahan" becomes by the end "May he show forth His might in saving Kathaleen Ny-Houlahan." Repetition has a kind of incremental effect apart from the refrain also. "Long they pine in weary woe the nobles of our land/Long they wander to and fro, proscribed, alas! and banned." And the characteristic alliteration and assonance can be readily seen as well. The alliterative long line is again an adaptation of the line used by the *filid,* discussed earlier:

> Long they pine in weary woe, the nobles of our land,
> Long they wander to and fro, proscribed, alas! and banned;
> Feastless, houseless, altarless, they bear the exile's brand,
>   But their hope is in the coming-to of Kathaleen Ny-Houlahan!

> Think her not a ghostly hag, too hideous to be seen,
> Call her not unseemly names, our matchless Kathaleen;
> Young she is, and fair she is, and would be crowned a queen
>   Were the king's son at home here with Kathaleen Ny-Houlahan!

Sweet and mild would look her face, O, none so sweet and mild,
Could she crush the foes by whom her beauty is reviled;
Woolen plaids would grace herself and robes of silk her child,
    If the king's son were living here with Kathaleen Ny-Houlahan!

Sore disgrace it is to see the Arbitress of thrones,
Vassal to a *Saxoneen* of cold and sapless bones!
Bitter anguish wrings our souls — with heavy sighs and groans
    We wait the Young Deliverer of Kathaleen Ny-Houlahan!

Let us pray to Him who holds Life's issues in His hands —
Him who formed the mighty globe, with all its thousand lands;
Girding them with seas and mountains, rivers deep, and strands,
    To cast a look of pity upon Kathaleen Ny-Houlahan!

He, who over sands and waves led Israel along —
He, who fed, with heavenly bread, that chosen tribe and throng —
He, who stood by Moses, when his foes were fierce and strong —
    May He show forth His might in saving Kathaleen Ny-Houlahan.
                                         (16-17)

It is not primarily either the alliteration or assonance of this poem but the steady building of emotion, which comes from a similarity of structure in successive sentences, that gives a power and surge to the verse: "Think her not a ghostly hag too hideous to be seen/Call her not unseemly names, our matchless Kathaleen."

From the same year as "Kathaleen Ny-Houlahan" comes another Irish poem which precedes Mangan's involvement with *The Nation* and his serious study of the Irish language. "Kincora" or "Lamentation of MacLiag for Kincora" appeared in the *Irish Penny Journal* on January 9, 1841; and Mangan depended for its substance on O'Curry's prose translation. The poet, MacLiag, to whom it is probably erroneously attributed, was secretary of the great Brian Boru, and thus the historical setting of the poem is a much earlier one than that of the poems we have been considering.

Brian Boru was the only man ever able to establish himself as undisputed King of Ireland. The Irish tribal life was very like the Jewish tribal existence prior to Saul's being made king; and in such a society, however brave and warlike the tribe is, it is an easy prey to larger groups of invaders. One such group who invaded Ireland about the end of the eighth century was the Vikings; they took over the monasteries, founded the first Irish cities such as Dubh Linn (Black Pond), and amalgamated eventually with the Gaels; but the Vikings were in control of the country until Brian Boru united the tribes, left his fortress at Kincora, and died defeating the Vikings in 1014 at the famous Battle of Clontarf. He thereby broke the power of the Vikings not only in Ireland but also in Northern Europe. The poem is not one of Mangan's finest, but what beauty it has comes from his artistry and not from the original.[7] In the *ubi sunt* tradition, the poem recalls an eleventh-century Ireland in a poignant way:

> Oh, where, Kincora! is Brian the Great?
> And where is the beauty that once was thine?
> Oh, where are the princes and nobles that sate
> At the feast in thy halls, and drank the red wine?
> > Where, oh Kincora?

> Oh, where, Kincora! are thy valorous lords?
> Oh, whither, thou Hospitable! are they gone?
> Oh, where are the Dalcassians of the Golden Swords?
> And where are the warriors Brian led on?
> > Where, oh, Kincora?

> And where is Murrough, the descendant of kings —
> The defeater of a hundred — the daringly brave —
> Who set but slight store by jewels and rings —
> Who swam down the torrent and laughed at its wave?
> > Where, oh, Kincora?

> And where is Donogh, King Brian's worthy son?
> And where is Conaing, the Beautiful Chief?
> And Kian, and Corc? Alas! they are gone —
> They have left me this night alone with my grief!
> > Left me, Kincora!

> And where are the chiefs with whom Brian went forth,
> The ne'er-vanquished son of Evin the Brave,
> The great King of Onaght, renowned for his worth,
> And the hosts of Baskinn, from the western wave?
> > Where, oh, Kincora?

> Oh, where is Duvlann of the Swift-footed Steeds?
> And where is Kian, who was son of Molloy?

And where is King Lonergan, the fame of whose deeds
In the red battle-field no time can destroy?
                    Where, oh, Kincora?

And where is that youth of majestic height,
The faith-keeping Prince of the Scots? — Even he,
As wide as his fame was, as great as was his might,
Was tributary, oh, Kincora, to thee!
                    Thee, oh, Kincora!

They are gone, those heroes of royal birth,
Who plundered no churches, and broke no trust,
'Tis weary for me to be living on earth
When they, oh, Kincora, lie low in the dust!
                    Low, oh, Kincora!

Oh, never again will Princes appear,
To rival the Dalcassians of the Cleaving Swords!
I can never dream of meeting afar or anear,
In the east or the west, such heroes and lords!
                    Never, Kincora!

Oh, dear are the images my memory calls up
Of Brian Boru! — how he never would miss
To give me at the banquet the first bright cup!
Ah! why did he heap on me honour like this?
                    Why, oh, Kincora?

I am Mac Liag, and my home is on the Lake;
Thither often, to that palace whose beauty is fled,
Came Brian to ask me, and I went for his sake.
Oh, my grief! that I should live, and Brian be dead!
                    Dead, oh, Kincora!
                        (49-51)

The refrain which changes slightly from stanza to stanza is very effective, and the poem's antiquity impresses on the reader the long tradition of poetic lament in Ireland. It is as though poetry and lament are synonymous, tied up as is most Irish verse in a history which seems to have neither a beginning nor an end of suffering.

A *Nation* poem which deals with a later Irish hero, "A Farewell to Patrick Sarsfield, Earl of Lucan," appeared in this patriotic organ of the Young Ireland movement on October 24, 1846. Sarsfield was the hero of the ill-fated Battle of the Boyne in 1689; but, for the reader unfamiliar with Irish history, a little background is necessary. After a peasant's revolt in 1641 and a simultaneous, unsuccessful attempt by the Irish to take Dublin Castle, Irish chieftains and peasants turned on their oppressors and killed as many as ten thousand. To punish these acts Cromwell came to Ireland, but his arrival was delayed eight years by the Civil War in England. The Puritan zealot arrived in September, 1649, with twenty thousand men, took Drogheda, and slaughtered all its inhabitants as an example to potential insurrectionists; then he did the same in Wexford but left the final capitulation of Galway to his son-in-law, Ireton, in 1652. The confiscation of Irish lands went forward since "adventurers" had been promised land before coming to Ireland; but, while Cromwell originally thought that two and a half million acres would be enough, it was now necessary to take eleven million out of a general total of twenty million acres. Only Connaught and Clare were left to the original inhabitants.

With the accession of James II in 1685, a change of atmosphere and an attempt to rectify some of Cromwell's injustices occurred. However, the blatant Catholicism of James caused his downfall, and he was driven from the country in 1688. James went to France, returned to Ireland with seven thousand French soldiers, and landed at Kinsale in March, 1689. Nevertheless, when William of Orange arrived in Ireland with his thirty-six thousand German and Huguenot mercenaries, his numbers and his technical superiority proved too much for James and for the Irish. Patrick Sarsfield led the Irish forces, but his heroism was hardly matched by that of King James, who fled after six days, and the Battle of the Boyne saw the inevitable defeat of the Jacobites. In the moment of defeat, Sarsfield said: "Change kings and let us fight it over." Sarsfield was the first of the famous "Wild Geese," the exiled Irish soldiers fighting in every nation of Europe but their own; and Sarsfield is reported to have said when dying in battle in the Netherlands, "Oh that this were for Ireland." The poem is given in full:

> Farewell, O Patrick Sarsfield, may luck be on your path!
>   Your camp is broken up, your work is marred for years;
> But you go to kindle into flame the King of France's wrath
>   Though you leave sick Eire in tears —
>   Och, ochone!

May the white sun and moon rain glory on your head,
   All hero as you are, and holy man of God!
To you the Saxons owe a many an hour of dread
   In the land you have often trod —
                           Och, ochone!

The Son of Mary guard you, and bless you to the end!
   'Tis altered is the time when your legions were astir,
When at Cullen you were hailed as conqueror and friend,
   And you crossed Narrow-water, near Birr —
                           Och, ochone!

I'll journey to the north, over mount, moor, and wave;
   'Twas there I first beheld drawn up, in file and line,
The brilliant Irish hosts; they were bravest of the brave,
   But alas, they scorned to combine —
                           Och, ochone!

I saw the royal Boyne when his billows flashed with blood;
   I fought at Graine Og, when a thousand horsemen fell;
On the dark empurpled plain of Aughrim, too, I stood,
   On the plain by Tubberdonny's well —
                           Och, ochone!

To the heroes of Limerick, the city of the fights,
   Be my best blessing borne on the wings of the air;
We had card playing there o'er our camp fires at night,
   And the Word of Life, too, and prayer —
                           Och, ochone!

But for you, Londonderry, may plague smite and slay
   Your people, may ruin desolate you stone by stone!
Thro' you there's many a gallant youth lies coffinless today,
   With the winds for mourners alone —
                           Och, ochone!

I clomb the high hill on a fair summer noon,
   And saw the Saxons muster, clad in armour blinding bright:
Oh, rage withheld my hand, or gunsman and dragoon
   Should have supped with Satan that night! —
                           Och, ochone!

How many a noble soldier, how many a cavalier,
   Careered along this road, seven fleeting weeks ago,
With silver-hilted sword, with matchlock and with spear,

Who now, *mavrone!* lies low —
              Och, ochone!

All hail to thee, Ben Eder! but ah, on thy brow
  I see a limping soldier, who battled and who bled
Last year in the cause of the Stuart, though now
  The worthy is begging his bread —
              Och, ochone!

And Diarmid, O Diarmid! he perished in the strife;
  His head it was spiked upon a halberd high;
His colours they were trampled: he had no chance of life
  If the Lord God Himself stood by! —
              Och, ochone!

But most, O my woe! I lament and lament
  For the ten valiant heroes who dwelt nigh the Nore,
And my three blessed brothers; they left me and went
  To the wars, and returned no more —
              Och, ochone!

On the bridge of the Boyne was our first overthrow;
  By Slavery the next, for we battled without rest;
The third was at Aughrim. O Eire! thy woe
  Is a sword in my bleeding breast —
              Och, ochone!

Oh, the roof above our heads, it was barbarously fired,
  While the black Orange guns blazed and bellowed around!
And as volley followed volley, Colonel Mitchel inquired
  Whether Lucan still stood his ground? —
              Och, ochone!

But O'Kelly still remains, to defy and to toil,
  He has memories that hell won't permit him to forget,
And a sword that will make the blue blood flow like oil
  Upon many an Aughrim yet! —
              Och, ochone!

And I never shall believe that my fatherland can fall
  With the Burkes, and the Decies, and the son of Royal James
And Talbot, the captain, and Sarsfield above all,
  The beloved of damsels and dames —
              Och, ochone!
               (80-83)

The poem's form is similar to that of "Kincora," a kind of ballad stanza with a fifth line serving as a short moan. The lament is much less formal than in "Lament for the Princes of Tyrone and Tyrconnell," and it opens with a farewell to the hero who has fled to France after the defeat at the Boyne, then moves by the end to a stronger if somewhat wistful hope that "I never shall believe that my fatherland can fall" with men of the stamp of Sarsfield.

The poem's use of the first person reminds us of Walt Whitman's similar use of first person with much broader implications, as when Mangan writes, "I saw the royal Boyne when his billows flashed with blood;/ I fought at Graine Og, when a thousand horsemen fell." And Padraic Colum has said of Mangan's poem that it "has behind it more humanity than is behind the rest of Mangan's verse."

A week after "A Farewell to Patrick Sarsfield" had appeared in *The Nation,* Mangan published another patriotic poem in the same magazine. "Lament for Banba" was originally titled "A Cry for Ireland," and it is derived from the Irish of Egan O'Rahilly, an early eighteenth-century "peasant imitator" of the former bards, and one of the best such imitators. The name "Banba" is another of the ancient names for Ireland:

> O my land! O my love!
>   What a woe, and how deep,
> Is thy death to my long mourning soul!
> God alone, God above,
>   Can awake thee from sleep,
> Can release thee from bondage and dole!
>   Alas, alas, and alas!
>   For the once proud people of Banba!
>
> As a tree in its prime,
>   Which the axe layeth low,
> Didst thou fall, O unfortunate land!
> Not by Time, nor thy crime,
>   Came the shock and the blow.
> They were given by a false felon hand!
>   Alas, alas, and alas!
>   For the once proud people of Banba!
>
> O, my grief of all griefs,
>   Is to see how thy throne
> Is usurped, whilst thyself art in thrall!
> Other lands have their chiefs,

Have their kings, thou alone
Art a wife, yet a widow withal!
Alas, alas, and alas!
For the once proud people of Banba!

The high house of O'Neill
Is gone down to the dust,
The O'Brien is clanless and banned;
And the steel, the red steel,
May no more be the trust
Of the Faithful and Brave in the land!
Alas, alas, and alas!
For the once proud people of Banba!

True, alas! Wrong and Wrath
Were of old all too rife.
Deeds were done which no good man admires;
And perchance Heaven hath
Chastened us for the strife
And the blood-shedding ways of our sires!
Alas, alas, and alas!
For the once proud people of Banba!

But, no more! This our doom,
While our hearts yet are warm,
Let us not over-weakly deplore!
For the hour soon may loom
When the Lord's mighty hand
Shall be raised for our rescue once more!
And our grief shall be turned into joy
For the still proud people of Banba!
(41-43)

Professor James Kilroy, in speaking of Mangan's patriotic poetry, has made a useful distinction between the public and the personal poetry. The personal we have been conditioned to analyze in the manner of New Critics, who seek paradox, irony, and subtle effects which are not, and cannot be, the concern of public poetry:

Public poetry, in which rhetorical techniques are used to move or convince a wide audience, and in which subtlety is not a necessary virtue — this large and respectable body of poetry evades our modern approaches. The problem is apparent in the later poetry of Mangan's contemporary, Alfred Lord Tennyson. The genuine power of his patriotic poems is not usually denied, but the obvious subjects and obtrusive sentiments of "The Charge of the Light Brigade" or "Ode on the Death of the Duke of Wellington" do not attract our literary critics. And yet, the proven and lasting appeal of Tennyson's public poems, and Kipling's as well, should make us find the method and the terms by which to analyze them. Undeniably Mangan's patriotic poems, like those of these English poets, lack internal subtlety. But since their intention is to bestir a wide audience to confidence in their nation or to remind them of Ireland's sorrows, subtlety may be sacrificed to other effects.[8]

"Lament for Banba" seems typical of such "public" poetry. When read silently by the private reader, its rhythm might seem too trotting and inflexible for its meaning. When read aloud publicly, the poem might not completely escape such an indictment, but its incantatory power, so typical of Mangan's work, is more evident. Furthermore, the poem's regularity of meter and of stanza, as well as its use of refrain, suit a public lament. The stanzas are similar in form — lines one, two, four, and five have two feet of anapests; lines three and six, three such feet; and lines seven and eight are the refrain. Unnecessary monotony is avoided by having varied line length, and proper repetition and tediousness, to be expected in a lament, are given by the regularity and refrain. When the refrain is finally altered in the last stanza from "Alas, alas, and alas!/For the once proud people of Banba!" to "And our grief shall be turned into joy/For the still proud people of Banba!" the poem can end on a note of optimism. The Lord's chastisement of the fifth stanza (a note of moderation for a patriotic poem since it grants Irish excesses) gives way to the Lord's rescue in the final stanza. Perhaps not one of Mangan's finest poems, "Lament for Banba" possesses much of Mangan's genius for musical effect.

In 1847, Mangan published in the *Dublin University Magazine* "Ellen Bawn," a love poem written essentially in hexameter couplets. As that very meter might suggest, the theme of this "translation" from an anonymous Irish source is treated somewhat humorously:

Ellen Bawn, O Ellen Bawn, you darling, darling dear, you,
Sit awhile beside me here, I'll die unless I'm near you!
'Tis for you I'd swim the Suir and breast the Shannon's waters;
For, Ellen dear, you've not your peer in Galway's blooming daughters!

Had I Limerick's gems and gold at will to mete and measure,
Were Loughrea's abundance mine, and all Portumna's treasure

These might lure me, might insure me many and many a new love,
But O! no bribe could pay your tribe for one like you, my true love!

Blessings be on Connaught! that's the place for sport and raking!
Blessing, too, my love, on you, a-sleeping and a-waking!
I'd have met you, dearest Ellen, when the sun went under,
But, woe! the flooding Shannon broke across my path in thunder!

Ellen! I'd give all the deer in Limerick's parks and arbours,
Ay, and all the ships that rode last year in Munster's harbours,
Could I blot from Time the hour I first became your lover,
For, O! you've given my heart a wound it never can recover!

Would to God that in the sod my corpse to-night were lying,
And the wild birds wheeling o'er it, and the winds a-sighing,
Since your cruel mother and your kindred choose to sever
Two hearts that Love would blend in one for ever and for ever!

                                                                (43-44)

This poem has provoked surprisingly different reactions. Guiney praised it because "its vehemence and incoherence stamp it as genuinely felt, as well as genuinely conceived."[9] On the other hand, Kilroy has faulted it for having a rhythm that distracts from its love theme.[10] If, however, the reader sees that the poet treats the love with tongue-in-cheek humor, the charges of incoherence and of inappropriate rhythm give way. Mangan could hardly have been serious or personal when writing a line such as "Blessings be on Connaught! that's the place for sport and raking." Likewise, the major incoherency that Guiney sees — the speaker's wanting to swim the Shannon for his love (1.3) and his inability because of its flooding (1.12) — is one of the most humorous twists of the poem. Having offered to play Leander for his Hero, he very unheroically is thwarted by a flood. Mangan's love of strong rhythm, which very often can work havoc with his meaning, is well suited to his purposes in this poem because of its very inappropriateness to a love theme. The hyperboles and the already mentioned couplet form also lend to the wit. All of this is not to say that Mangan is not also serious about the love element of the poem, but rather to point out that "Ellen Bawn" is another example of what Chesterton regarded as the older Irish tradition of passing from the humorous to the serious within the same poem.

A late poem, one different in theme, is "St. Patrick's Hymn

Before Tara." Published in the *Irish Catholic Magazine* in February, 1848, the poem is a prayer attributed to St. Patrick at the great center of Druidism, Tara. The saint calls upon the Triune God and all his heavenly saints to protect him from the powers of Darkness in this pagan shrine. Patrick had arrived in Ireland in 432 with the twofold intention of converting the Gaels from paganism and the influence of the Druids and of establishing a Roman Christianity with its smoothly functioning hierarchical system of dioceses, bishops, priests, laity, and so forth. In his first aim he was eminently successful, but in his second less so. Irish Christianity took its structural form not so much from St. Patrick as from St. Columkill in the sixth century when it became monastic rather than diocesan. This fact may seem a blessing in our age when the spirituality of monasteries often appears to stand in bold relief against dioceses that are frequently run by financiers rather than by spiritual men; and, in large part, monasticism was a blessing then because Ireland became famous for its scholarly and saintly monasteries which spread their culture throughout the Medieval world. On the other hand, Irish monastic spirituality did not serve as a leaven among the unscholarly community in the way a diocesan clergy could have, for the monks lived like hermits, quite apart from even one another.

Mangan was not normally very successful with religious subjects. Yet this poem has a litanylike repetitiveness which builds to a powerful crescendo:

> At Tara to-day in this awful hour,
>   I call on the Holy Trinity!
> Glory to Him who reigneth in power,
> The God of the elements, Father and Son,
> And Paraclete Spirit, which Three are the One,
>   The ever-existing Divinity!
>
> At Tara to-day I call on the Lord,
> On Christ the Omnipotent Word,
> Who came to redeem from Death and Sin
>   Our fallen race;
>   And I put and I place
> The virtue that lieth and liveth in
>   His Incarnation lowly,
>   His Baptism pure and holy,
> His life of toil, and tears, and affliction,
> His dolorous Death — His Crucifixion,

His Burial, sacred and sad and lone,
    His Resurrection to life again.
His glorious Ascension to Heaven's high Throne,
And lastly, his future dread
    And terrible coming to judge all men —
    Both the Living and Dead. . . .

At Tara to-day I put and I place
    The virtue that dwells in the Seraphim's love,
And the virtue and grace
        That are in the obedience
        And unshaken allegiance
Of all the Archangels and angels above,
And in the hope of the Resurrection
To everlasting reward and election,
And in the prayers of the Fathers of old,
And in the truths the Prophets foretold,
And in the Apostles' manifold preachings,
And in the Confessor's faith and teachings,
And in the purity ever dwelling
        Within the Immaculate Virgin's breast,
And in the actions bright and excelling
    Of all good men, the just and the blest. . . .

At Tara to-day, in this fateful hour,
I place all Heaven with its power,
And the sun with its brightness,
And the snow with its whiteness,
And fire with all the strength it hath,
And lightning with its rapid wrath,
And the winds with their swiftness along their path,
And the sea with its deepness,
And the rocks with their steepness,
And the earth with its starkness,
        All these I place,
        By God's almighty help and grace,
Between myself and the Powers of Darkness.

        At Tara to-day
        May God be my stay!
May the strength of God now nerve me!
May the power of God preserve me!
May God the Almighty be near me!
    May God the Almighty espy me!
May God the Almighty hear me!

    May God give me eloquent speech!
May the arm of God protect me!
May the wisdom of God direct me!
    May God give me power to teach and to preach!

May the shield of God defend me!
May the host of God attend me,
    And ward me,
    And guard me,
Against the wiles of demons and devils,
Against the temptations of vices and evils,
Against the bad passions and wrathful will
    Of the reckless mind and the wicked heart
Against every man who designs me ill,
    Whether leagued with others or plotting apart!

    In this hour of hours,
    I place all those powers
Between myself and every foe,
    Who threaten my body and soul
    With danger or dole,
To protect me against the evils that flow
From lying soothsayers' incantations,
From the gloomy laws of the Gentile nations,
From Heresy's hateful innovations,
From Idolatry's rites and invocations,
    Be those my defenders,
    My guards against every ban,
And spells of smiths and Druids, and women;
In fine, against every knowledge that renders
    The light Heaven sends us dim in
        The spirit and soul of Man!
        May Christ, I pray,
        Protect me to-day
    Against poison and fire
    Against drowning and wounding,
That so, in His grace abounding,
    I may earn the Preacher's hire!

    Christ, as a light,
    Illumine and guide me!
Christ, as a shield, o'ershadow and cover me
Christ be under me! Christ be over me!
    Christ be beside me
    On left hand and right!

Christ be before me, behind me, about me!
Christ this day be within and without me!

Christ the lowly and meek,
   Christ, the All-powerful, be
In the heart of each to whom I speak,
   In the mouth of each who speaks to me!
      In all who draw near me,
      Or see or hear me!

At Tara to-day, in this awful hour,
   I call on the Holy Trinity!
Glory to Him who reigneth in power,
The God of the Elements, Father and Son,
And Paraclete Spirit, which Three are the One,
      The ever-existing Divinity!

Salvation dwells with the Lord,
With Christ, the Omnipotent Word.
From generation to generation,
Grant us, O Lord, thy grace and salvation!
                                    (44-48)

The words "At Tara" which open most stanzas are not in the
original that Mangan "translated." Yet the mention of the town,
twenty miles from Dublin, conjures up a past like that of
Stonehenge; and the founder of Irish Christianity looms like Moses
against the Egyptian priests in his call upon God to be with him in
the face of these hostile pagans.

CHAPTER 4

Original Poems

I *The Youthful Poet*

THE group of poems which O'Donoghue calls "original" comprises those which Mangan makes no pretext of having translated. There are as many successful ones among these poems as among the "translations," and they reaffirm Mangan's original genius. Among the earliest of these original poems is one which he wrote at sixteen, though it was not published until thirty years later when the fragment appeared in the *Irishman* on June 23, 1849 — the day Mangan was buried. The poem, "Genius," is indicative of the youngster's sense of isolation, even persecution; and it is shot through with a kind of Shelleyan idealism which may not be accidental. Young Mangan may even have heard Shelley speak a few years earlier when he had appeared in Mangan's neighborhood as part of his effort to liberate the Irish.

> O Genius! Genius! all thou dost endure,
> First from thyself, and finally from those
> The earth-bound and the Blind, who cannot feel
> That there be souls with purposes as pure
> And lofty as the mountain snows, and zeal
> All quenchless as the spirit whence it flows.
>
> (172)

These lines reflect the youngster's lonely situation in his family which did not understand his bibliophilia and understood even less his chagrin at working in the scrivener's office. Nevertheless, the lines seem to have been written by a young poet thoroughly familiar not only with Shelley and his *Epipsychidion* but also with Byron, Mangan's favorite.

Equally imitative, if somewhat more mature, is a poem written for

The Comet in 1832, "Lines on the Death of a Beloved Friend." The
death of Mangan's young student of German, Catherine Hayes,
seems to have occasioned the poem, but the poem dwells very little
on her death. Instead, it congratulates her for escaping "the tears
and woe,/And deaths on deaths the living undergo"; and it does so in
the ironic way that Housman employs later in "To An Athlete Dying
Young." But Mangan's poem does not pursue this ironic cause for
happiness; it again focuses on the sufferings of those left to carry on,
particularly the poet:

> Thou diedst ere the icy breath of Scorn
> Froze the Warm feelings of thy girlhood's morn —
> Ere thou couldst learn that Man is but a slave,
> And this blank world a prison and a grave.
>
> Thy spirit is at peace — Peace! blessed word!
> Forgotten by the million — or unheard;
> But mine still struggles down this Vale of Death,
> And courts the favour of a little breath!
>
> Through every stage of Life's consuming fever
> The soul too often is her own deceiver,
> And revels — even in a world like this —
> In golden visions of unbounded bliss.
>   (134)

Nevertheless, as the poet begins to get lost in the Byronic pose he has
assumed, he recalls his purpose in this elegy and finds occasion
for optimism:

> But he who, looking on the naked chart
> Of Life, feels nature sinking at his heart,
> He who is drugged with sorrows, he for whom
> Affliction carves a pathway to the tomb,
>
> He will unite with me to bless that Power
> Who gathers and transplants the fragile flower
> Ere yet the spirit of the whirlwind storm
> Comes forth in wrath to prostrate and deform.
>
> And if it be that God Himself removes
> From peril and contagion those He loves,

> Weep such no more — but strew with freshest roses
> The hallowed mound where Innocence reposes.
>
> (134)

Having shown, however, that his main concern is the deceased, this persistent Byronic soul returns in the final stanza to his own loss and blends this strain with the elegiac counterpart:

> The world is round me now, but sad and single
> I stand amid the throng with whom I mingle;
> Not one of all of whom can be to me
> The bosom treasure I have lost in thee.
>
> (135)

The month that Mangan turned thirty, he published in the *Irish Penny Journal* a ballad entitled "The One Mystery," an eight-line ballad stanza or compression of two stanzas in the mode of Wordsworth, which is used, as are many of Mangan's ballads, to treat a philosophical problem. The problem is the eternally gnawing question of what lies beyond life. We cannot know the answer. Neither the past, nor wisdom, nor science can convey an answer. The earth might be a kind of Wordsworthian or Neoplatonic type of what has been and what will be in some other existence:

> Supposest thou the wondrous powers,
>   To high imagination given,
> Pale types of what shall yet be ours,
>   When earth is heaven?
> When this decaying shell is cold,
>   Oh! sayest thou the soul shall climb
> That magic mount she trod of old,
>   Ere childhood's time?

Yet his answer is somewhat pessimistic or at least, as in Shelley's *Epipsychidion*, doubtful of the value of standard, facile religious solutions:

> No more, no more — with aching brow
>   And restless heart, and burning brain,
> We ask the When, the Where, the How,
>   And ask in vain.
> And all philosophy, all faith,

All earthly — all celestial lore,
Have but one voice, which only saith —
    Endure — adore!
        (123-24)

The stanzas quoted are not a sample of the best in the poem, but they do give an indication even at this early date of Mangan's religious thought. He is closer to Shelley than to the orthodox Catholicism that most of his biographers attribute to him as a lifelong characteristic. The final word, "adore," perhaps indicates a belief in some supreme power, and Mangan might never have lost such a belief. On the other hand, since the word is the only such reference in the poem, it might simply be taken as the advice of "all earthly and celestial lore" of whose limitations as teachers the poem has already assured us.

From this same year which found Mangan given to opium comes another pessimistic and more poignant work called "A Broken-Hearted Lay," which was written for *The Comet:*

Weep for one blank, one desert epoch in
    The history of the heart; it is the time
When all which dazzled us no more can win;
    When all that beamed of starlike and sublime
Wanes, and we stand lone mourners o'er the burial
    Of perished pleasure, and a pall funeral,
Stretching afar across the hueless heaven,
    Curtains the kingly glory of the sun,
    And robes the melancholy earth in one
Wide gloom: when friends for whom we could have striven
With pain, and peril, and the sword, and given
Myriads of lives, had such been merged in ours,
    Requite us with falseheartedness and wrong;
When sorrows haunt our path like evil powers,
    Sweeping and countless as the legion throng.

Then, when the unbroken dreams of boyhood's span,
    And when the inanity of all things human,
And when the dark ingratitude of man,
    And when the hollower perfidy of woman,
Come down like night upon the feelings, turning
    This rich, bright world, so redolent of bloom,
Into a lazar-house of tears and mourning —
    Into the semblance of a living tomb!

When, yielding to the night she cannot master
    The soul forsakes her palace halls of youth,
    And (touched by the Ithuriel wand of truth,
Which oft in one brief hour works wonders vaster
Than those of Egypt's old magician host)
Sees at a single glance that all is lost!
And brooding in her cold and desolate lair
Over the phantom-wreck of things that were,
    And asking destiny if nought remain?
    Is answered — bitterness and life-long pain,
Remembrance, and reflection, and despair,
    And torturing thoughts that will not be forbidden,
    And agonies that cannot all be hidden!
                  (124-25)

This year of 1833 was one of great personal sorrow for Mangan. The love affair with Margaret Stackpoole was terminated and Sheehan's attacks on Mangan as a drunkard, printed in his own paper, forced the poet to leave *The Comet*. The poem, therefore, seems an unburdening of personal hurt in a way Mangan was not given to in his prose or in his poetic "translations."

The basic iambic pentameter is broken frequently, thus isolating and emphasizing ideas and feeling as though they could not be contained within a framework of normal expression. We note, for example, the irregularity of the opening line before the poet settles into the more regular iambs of the second and third lines. Also noteworthy in lending the poem its artistic power is Mangan's standard use of incremental repetition that builds up to emotional climax. It is evident in the first four lines of the second stanza, but also throughout the same stanza, as when he cries, "Into a lazar-house of tears and mourning — /Into the semblance of a living tomb!" The second stanza is one long sentence which grows in power as it builds to its conclusion. Likewise, the opening stanza is essentially one lengthy sentence ending with the betrayed friendship that casts such a pall over the beauty of this earth. The poem's feelings recall Wordsworth's and Coleridge's reflections on joy, the former in his insistence that it is joy which is the stuff of poetry and of vision, the latter in "Dejection! An Ode," where he demonstrates how the absence of joy has robbed him of his poetic gift.

II   *The Mature Poet*

If we skip the seven years during which Mangan devoted much of his time to Oriental translations, we find a poem that shows considerable religious development since "The One Mystery." The inspiration for "Life and Its Illusions," published in the *Irish Penny Journal* on August 22, 1840, was drawn from Edward Young who furnishes the motto. The poem has much of the Platonism of "The One Mystery." We are shadows, and our lives are more unreal than dreams:

> We are but shadows! None of all those things,
> Formless and vague, that flit upon the wings
> Of wild Imagination round thy couch,
> When Slumber seals thine eyes, is clothed with such
> An unreality as Human Life,
> Cherished and clung to as it is; . . .
>
> (135)

The Platonism here, however, is subsumed by orthodox Christianity or something much closer to it than the earlier "One Mystery" had demonstrated. Mangan refers to the Supreme Being as "Ancient of Days" (a biblical title) and as the "First Cause" (a Thomistic title) whose "name is Love" and whose "word is Truth." Furthermore, he does suggest that the unreality of things human, the worthlessness of hope and striving in this life, might be offset by the "one imperishable crown" that practicers of the Christian beatitudes will find in the next life:

> Ancient of Days! First Cause! Adored! Unknown!
> Who wert, and art, and art to come! The heart
> Yearns, in its lucid moods, to Thee alone!
> Thy name is Love; thy word is Truth; thou art
> The Fount of Happiness — the source of Glory —
> Eternity is in thy hands, and Power.
> Oh, from that sphere unrecognised by our
> Slow souls, look down upon a world which, hoary
> In Evil and in Error though it be,
> Retains even yet some trace of that primeval
> Beauty that bloomed upon its brow ere Evil
> And Error wiled it from Thy Love and Thee!
> Look down, and if, while human brows are brightening
> In godless triumph, angel eyes be weeping,
> Publish Thy will in syllables of lightning
> And sentences of thunder to the Sleeping!
> Look down, and renovate the waning name
> Of Goodness, and relume the waning light

Of Truth and Purity! — that all may aim
At one imperishable crown — the bright
Guerdon which they who by untired and holy
Exertion overcome the world, inherit —
The Self-denying, the Peaceable, the Lowly,
The truly Merciful, the Poor in spirit!

So shall the end of thine all-perfect plan
At length be realised in erring Man.
                                    (136-37)

The poem's form is interesting. Though in places it seems straight-forward iambic couplets with run-on lines, the rhyme scheme often alternates an *abab* pattern or goes to an *abba* scheme. This scheme gives him almost as much freedom as blank verse while satisfying Mangan's love for sound:

And well may earth-directed zeal be blighted!
And well may Time laugh selfish hopes to scorn!
He lives in vain whose reckless years have slighted
The humbling truth which Penitence and grey
Hairs teach the Wise, that such cold hopes are born
Only to dupe and to be thus requited!
How many such there be! — in whom the thorn
Which Disappointment plants festers in vain,
Save as the instrument of sleepless pain —
Who bear about with them the burning feeling
And fire of that intolerable word
Which, inly searching, pierceth, like a sword,
The breast whose wounds thence forward know no healing!
                                    (136)

Not only is the enjambment and freedom with rhyme scheme evident in these verses, but the characteristic power of Mangan which gains so much from incremental repetition is also evident in the first two lines.

A very curious and witty poem is one which Mangan wrote in 1844 for the *Dublin University Magazine*. He gave it to *The Nation* five years later as though it had never before been published, and he once again attributed it to "Selber." The poem, "The Coming Event," is filled with irony about the need to renounce wine because judgment is at hand:

> Curtain the lamp, and bury the bowl —
> The ban is on drinking!
> Reason shall reign the queen of the soul
> When the spirits are sinking.
> (143)

After enhancing such a gloomy prospect through a stanza and a half more in words which the Puritan will take for a paean of praise to the Coming Event, he ironically concludes, "So should it be! — for Man's world of romance/Is fast disappearing." But, though the poem's irony is made evident in this line, the poet continues through another two stanzas in traditionally orthodox terms in which he prepares the believer for the Coming Event in such a way that the Last Judgment and the Frightening Prospect of Prohibition become blended:

> Darken the lamp, then, and bury the bowl,
> Ye Faithfullest-hearted!
> And, as your swift years hasten on to the goal
> Whither worlds have departed,
> Spend all, sinew, soul, in your zeal to atone
> For the past and its errors;
> So best shall ye bear to encounter alone
> the EVENT and its terrors
> (144)

The irony is not obtrusive, but it is evident in the poet who regards the new Puritanism as bringing with it romance's disappearance, who sees the spirits sinking as a corollary of the new reign of reason, and who bemoans the descent of night without the accompaniment of revelry: "Nights shall descend, and no taverns ring/To the roar of our revels." The poet who can joke about his Last Judgment as being the ban on drinking is more human and humorous than the poet who has been pictured as a paragon of orthodoxy, as an ever-steadfast Catholic rewarded at the end for his perseverance in the faith despite a life of great suffering.[1] Nevertheless, O'Donoghue failed to see the sinking of the spirits and the disappearance of romance as a thing not desired by the poet, and he read the poem straightforwardly as a formal abjuration of alcohol![2] The form is once again the eight-line ballad stanza, or juxtaposition of two ballad stanzas; and the ballad form acts as a better vehicle for such humor than it often has for his heavier lyrics.

A poem which represents a more traditional approach to religion or, better, philosophy, is "Khidder," which Mangan published in the *Dublin University Magazine* in 1845. Though not a "translation," the poem looks Oriental in theme as well as in title. Khidder is the Eastern name of Elijah; and, like the tradition that Elijah returns to earth from time to time, Khidder revisits the world every thousand years to check on man. He finds, when he does, that the earth is completely changed each time he passes a particular spot. A city gives way to pasture land; pasture land to lakes; and lakes to woods. Yet each time the inhabitants think their present world an eternal one. Finally, after four changes, the place returns to being a city:

> Thus said or sung
> Khidder, the ever-young: —
> Journeying, I passed an ancient town —
> Of lindens green its battlements bore a crown,
> And at its turreted gates, on either hand,
> Did fountains stand,
> In marble white of rarest chiselling,
> The which on high did fling
> Water, that then like rain went twinkling down,
> With a rainbow glancing in the spray
> As it wreathed in the sunny ray.
> I marked where, 'neath the frown
> Of the dark rampart, smiled a garden fair;
> And an old man was there,
> That gathered fruit. "Good father," I began,
> "Since when, I pray you, standeth here
> This goodly city with its fountains clear?"
> To which that agèd man
> Made answer — "Ever stood
> The city where it stands to-day,
> And as it stands so shall it stand for aye,
> Come evil days or good."
>
> Him gathering fruit I left, and journeyed on;
> But when a thousand years were come and gone,
> Again I passed that way, and lo!
> There was no city, there were no
> Fountains of chiselling rare,
> No garden fair,
> Only
> A lonely
> Shepherd was piping there,

Whose little flock seemed less
In that wide pasture of the wilderness.

"Good friend," quoth I,
"How long hath the fair city passed away,
That stood with gates so high,
With fountains bright, and gardens gay,
Where now these sheep do stray?"
And he replied — "What withers makes but room
For what springs up in verdurous bloom —
Sheep have grazed ever here, and here will graze for aye."

Him piping there I left, and journeyed on;
But when a thousand years were come and gone,
Again I passed
That way, and see! there was a lake
That darkened in the blast,
And waves that brake
With a melancholy roar
Along that lonely shore.
And on a shingly point that ran
Far out into the lake, a fisherman
Was hauling in his net. To him I said:
"Good friend,
I fain would know
Since when it is that here these waters flow?"
Whereat he shook his head,
— And answer made, "Heaven lend
Thee better wit, good brother! Ever here
These waters flowed, and so
Will ever flow:
And aye in this dark rolling wave
Men fished, and still fish,
And ever will fish,
Until fish
No more in waters swim."

Him
Hauling his net I left, and journeyed on;
But when a thousand years were come and gone,
Again I passed that way, and lo! there stood,
Where waves had rolled, a green and flourishing wood —
Flourishing in youth it seemed, and yet was old —
And there it stood where deep blue waves had rolled.
A place of pleasant shade!
A wandering wind among the branches played,

And birds were now where fish had been;
And through the depth of green,
In many a gush the golden sunshine streamed;
And wild flowers gleamed
About the brown and mossy
Roots of the ancient trees,
And the cushioned sward so glossy
That compassed these.

Here, as I passed, there met
Me, on the border of that forest wide,
One with an axe, whom, when I spied,
Quoth I — "Good neighbour, let
Me ask, I pray you, how long hath this wood
Stood,
Spreading its covert, broad and green,
Here, where mine eyes have seen
A royal city stand, whose battlements
Were like the ancient rocks;
And then a place for shepherds' tents,
And pasturage of flocks;
And then,
Roughening beneath the blast,
A vast
Dark mere — a haunt of fishermen?"

There was a cold surprise
In the man's eyes
While thus I spoke, and, as I made an end,
This was his dry
Reply —
"Facetious friend,
This wood
Hath ever stood
Even where it stands to-day;
And as it stands, so shall it stand for aye.
And here men catch no fish — here tend
No sheep — to no town-markets wend;
But aye in these
Green shades men felled, and still fell,
And ever will fell
Trees."

Him with his axe I left, and journeyed on;
But when a thousand years were come and gone,

Again I passed
That way; and lo! a town —
And spires, and domes, and towers looked proudly down
Upon a vast
And sounding tide of life,
That flowed through many a street and surged
In many a market-place, and urged
Its way in many a wheeling current, hither
And thither.
How rose the strife
Of sounds! the ceaseless beat
Of feet!
The noise of carts, of whips — the roll
Of chariots, coaches, cabs, gigs — (all
Who keep the last-named vehicle we call
Respectable) — horse-tramplings, and the toll
Of bells; the whirl, the clash, the hubbub-mingling
Of voices, deep and shrill; the clattering, jingling,
The indescribable, indefinable roar;
The grating, creaking, booming, clanking, thumping
And bumping,
And stumping
Of folks with wooden legs; the gabbling,
And babbling,
And many more
Quite nameless helpings
To the general effect; dog-yelpings,
Laughter, and shout, and cry; all sounds of gladness,
Of sadness,
And madness, —
For there were people marrying,
And others carrying
The dead they would have died for to the grave —
(Sadly the church bell tolled
When the young men were burying the old —
More sadly spake that bodeful tongue
When the old were burying the young) —
Thus did the tumult rave
Through that fair city — nor were wanting there
Of dancing dogs or bear,
Or need knife-
Grinder, or man with dismal wife,
That sang deplorably of *"purling groves*
And verdant streams, all where young Damon roves
With tender Phillida, the nymph he loves,

And softly breathe
The balmy moonbeam's wreathe,
And amorous turtle-doves" —
Or other doleful men, that blew
The melancholiest tunes — the which they only knew —
On flutes and other instruments of wind;
Or small dark imps, with hurdy-
Gurdy,
And marmoset, that grinned
For nuts, and might have been his brother,
They were so like each other;
Or man
That danced like the god Pan,
Twitching
A spasmy face
From side to side with a grace
Bewitching,
The while he whistled
In sorted pipes, all at his chin that bristled;
Or fiddler, fiddling much
For little profit, and many such
Street musics most forlorn
In that too pitiless rout quite overborne.

Now, when as I beheld
The crowd, and heard the din of life once more
Swell, as it swelled
In that same place four thousand years before,
I asked of them that passed me in the throng
How long
The city thereabouts had stood,
And what was gone with pasture, lake, and wood;
But at such question most men did but stare,
And so pass on; and some did laugh and shake
Their heads, me deeming mad; but none would spare
The time, or take
The pains to answer me, for there
All were in haste — all busy — bent to make
The most of every minute,
And do, an if they might, an hour's work in it.

Yet as I gave not o'er, but pertinaciously
Plied with my question every passer-by,
A dozen voices did at length reply
Ungraciously —

"What ravest thou
Of pasture, lake, and wood? As it is now
So was it always here, and so will be for aye."
Them, hurrying there, I left, and journeyed on —
But when a thousand years are come and gone,
Again I'll pass that way.
                              (163-69)

The poem is a rare experiment by Mangan with what is almost free verse. It has, of course, his trademarks, such as alliteration and assonance, internal rhyme, and a kind of refrain in each section which is an incremental repetition, leading to the forceful conclusion: "But when a thousand years are come and gone/Again I'll pass that way." The use of such devices as alliteration and internal rhyme gives a structure to verse that operates apart from meter and end rhyme. It was used by the early Irish bards; and Mangan either learned it from the new translations or, following Coleridge, learned the old Anglo-Saxon meter. It is noteworthy, however, that Mangan, in one of his few narrative poems, uses a verse which moves the story quickly yet preserves the music which is his trademark.

In 1846, Mangan began to contribute frequently to *The Nation,* the organ of the radical "Young Ireland" group which found the aging Daniel O'Connell no longer effective. At this time Mangan became political — or as political as it was in his nature to become, perhaps more than Joyce but less than Yeats. At any rate, he unquestionably emerged in this year as the national poet of Ireland with such things as "Dark Rosaleen," "The Dream of John MacDonnell," "A Vision of Connaught in the Thirteenth Century," and the great "Ode to the Maguire."

"A Vision of Connaught in the Thirteenth Century" is an Irish poem which is not a translation. It was published in *The Nation* on July 11, 1846, and is interesting not only for its own intrinsic beauty but also for its likenesses to Coleridge's "Kubla Khan." The persona refers to his lord as "Khan" in the second stanza, though the title is quite natural an anglicization of the Irish *Ceann,* or chief. The third stanza, however, presents a very Coleridgean vision in which a Dome reminiscent of Kubla's appears as well as "ancestral voices." Cahal Mor is certain to remind the reader of Kubla Khan too. O'Donoghue, though he does not discuss the English poet's influence on "A Vision of Connaught in the Thirteenth Century," does mention a letter to Duffy discussing a dream Mangan had in which the poet says "there was a light and a throng — not the 'lurid light and trampling throng' of Coleridge, yet quite as impressive."[3] However, Coleridge's poem played no larger a part in Mangan's than *Purchas' Pilgrimage* had in Coleridge's poem. Mangan used whatever he borrowed very effectively, and his poem has a theme and rhythm that are very much his own:

> I walked entranced
>   Through a land of Morn;
> The sun, with wondrous excess of light,
>   Shone down and glanced
>   Over seas of corn
> And lustrous gardens aleft and right.
>   Even in the clime
>   Of resplendent Spain,
> Beams no such sun upon such a land;
>   But it was the time,
>   'Twas in the reign,
> Of Cáhal Mór of the Wine-red Hand.
>
>   Anon stood nigh
>   By my side a man
> Of princely aspect and port sublime.
>   Him queried I —
>   "O, my Lord and Khan,
> What clime is this, and what golden time?"
>   When he — "The clime
>   Is a clime to praise,
> The clime is Erin's, the green and bland;
>   And it is the time
>   These be the days
> Of Cáhal Mór of the Wine-red Hand!"
>
>   Then saw I thrones,
>   And circling fires,
> And a Dome rose near me, as by a spell,
>   Whence flowed the tones
>   Of silver lyres,
> And many voices in wreathèd swell;
>   And their thrilling chime
>   Fell on mine ears
> As the heavenly hymn of an angel-band —
>   "It is now the time,

These be the years
Of Cáhal Mór of the Wine-red Hand!"

I sought the hall,
And, behold! a change
From light to darkness, from joy to woe!
King, nobles, all,
Looked aghast and strange;
The minstrel-group sate in dumbest show!
Had some great crime
Wrought this dread amaze,
This terror? None seemed to understand
'Twas then the time
We were in the days,
Of Cáhal Mór of the Wine-red Hand.

I again walked forth;
But lo! the sky
Showed fleckt with blood, and an alien sun
Glared from the north,
And there stood on high,
Amid his shorn beams, a skeleton!
It was by the stream
Of the castled Maine,
One autumn eve, in the Teuton's land,
That I dreamed this dream
Of the time and reign
Of Cáhal Mór of the Wine-red Hand!
(94-96)

The time is a century after the coming of the Normans from England, but Connaught had not yet come under Norman control and never entirely did. The de Burghs (Burkes) were the first Normans to seize a portion of Connaught, and that was not until the thirteenth century. However, even then the O'Connors held on to a good amount of their ancient possessions in Connaught. Consequently, the poem sings of a still free land, a halcyon period; but the vision in the hall and the portentous scenes of the last stanza must be caused by the fear seizing the Irish as they view the beginning of seven centuries of vassalage to Norman and English overlords.

Most effective in giving the "Vision" its rhythm is Mangan's gift for refrain and incremental repetition. The refrain,

> But it was the time,
> 'Twas in the reign
> Of Cáhal Mór of the Wine-red Hand

gives, with its slight changes, a haunting conclusion to each stanza.

A rather interesting departure from such Irish themes is a Coleridgean call to Pantisocracy, to an ideal society, in the new world. Mangan's "An Invitation" is a call to friends of freedom to forsake their present clime; for Europe is effete: "Europe — Southern, Saxon, Celt — /Sits alone in tattered robe." Rome's star is burned out, Deutschland sleeps, Spain bleeds, and Poland is chained. And that refuge of the Romantic poets, Italy, "can but groan and vow" while "England lieth sick to death." So, like Southey and Coleridge before him, Mangan trumpets the call to the New World.

> Friends to Freedom! is't not time
> That your course were shaped at length?
> Wherefore stand ye loitering here?
> Seek some healthier, holier clime,
> Where your souls may grow in strength,
> And whence Love hath exiled Fear!
> (150)

This curious poem simultaneously calls for a return of Ireland to its past glory, and such ambivalence can perhaps best be explained by its being an occasional poem for the United States' Independence Day (it was published on July 4) since so many of his countrymen had sought American shores; but the poem may also reflect an ambivalence on the part of many of the Irish patriots. Their fellow countrymen were beginning to be driven by famine and English insensitivity to the United States at the rate of two hundred thousand a year. Would it be better to seek a clime which promised to be more amenable to freedom or to continue with their old dream? At any rate, the same oppressive British government that had made Coleridge flirt with visions of the Susquehanna did the same to Mangan.

Late in the previous year, 1845, Mangan had contributed to an obscure Irish magazine, *The Irish Monthly Magazine,* a simple song called "Counsel of a Cosmopolitan." Its theme is the need to trust in divine, and not in human, love. Faith in a supreme being is not a new expression in Mangan, whatever he thought of orthodox manifestations of such faith. However, he addressed "God" in this poem — not "Supreme Being," "Ancient of Days," "First Cause," or the other abstractions that he had addressed in "Life and Its Illusions" five years earlier. "Counsel of a Cosmopolitan" opens in the vein of Housman's "When I Was One and Twenty" or of Keats's "La Belle Dame Sans Merci":

> Give smiles and sighs alike to all,
>   Serve all, but love not any;
> Love's dangerous and delicious thrall
>   Hath been the tomb of many.

And the poem continues in this spirit of skepticism toward earthy love.

> Why pawn thy soul for one lone flower,
>   And slight the whole bright garland;
> Clarissa's eyes, Lucinda's bower,
>   Will fail thee in a far land!
>   (154-55)

The hudibrastic rhyme of the second and fourth lines of this stanza might have been learned at the feet of his master, Byron, or it might have come from the ancient *aird rinn* of the bard. Wherever Mangan learned the technique, such rhyme served him poorly for the same reason already mentioned in the discussion of "Cean-Salla": he achieves humor without intending to do so.

Mangan's forte was not narrative poetry, but he made an interesting and successful departure into this mode in his final year with a poem called "Gasparo Bandollo," which appeared in the *Dublin University Magazine* and which was apparently, like Browning's *The Ring and the Book,* based upon an actual, historical, Italian tragedy. In the poem, young Giambattista Bandollo is appealed to by a fleeing, wounded Italian patriot, Sevrini, to hide him or at least not to betray his hiding place on the Bandollo property; and the boy agrees. Shortly afterward, the Italian soldiers, in hot pursuit of the rebel, whose blood marks led them to the Bandollo place, confront Giambattista and ask where Sevrini is. Though there is a reward, it seems not to be the boy's concern; but, in fear and obedience to their command, he timidly points to the hiding place, and Sevrini is taken. Then remorse sets in. Giambattista is not upset because he feels he has done the wrong or right thing politically. It is the sight of Sevrini's bloodstains that impress on him the notion he has sent a man to his death.

In the evening, Gasparo returns and learns the truth when he questions the boy:

> "Oh, father!" cried the boy — then, wild
>   With terror of some dreadful doom,
> He gasped for breath. — "Speak, wretched child!
>   *Who* sought my asylum, and from *whom*?"
>   "O God! Sevrini!" — "From — " "The Sbirri."
> "The fugitive was wounded, weary?" —
> — "O, father! I — this dreary room — "
>   "And thou betrayedst him?" — "O Heaven!" —
> — "And thou betrayedst him?" — "I-only — "
> — "And thou betrayedst him?" "O hear me,
> My father! I watch here so lonely
> All day, and feel, oh! so bereaven,
>   With not a sight or sound to cheer me!
> My mind — my — But, I only pointed —
> I spake not."
>   (147-48)

The father, in a fit of passion over the betrayal of this brave patriot, slays the boy. The final stanza, then, pictures Gasparo, fated to live long with neither a past nor a future to offer him much solace:

> Better thy child's lot had been thine —
>   The best lot after all! for Heaven
> Most careth for such weakling souls.
>   (149)

The poem is very effective, and it displays Mangan's ability in the narrative mode when he ventures in that direction. Much of the power comes again from Mangan's incremental repetition as seen, for example, in the lines above when the father, astonished, repeats his incredulous question about the boy's betrayal while the boy's brief response changes with each repetition of the question. Or we can see the same device in the final stanza in which the father's grief is described:

> A grief that speaks, albeit untold,
> And lives, where all seems dead and cold,

> And finds no refuge in the Past,
> And sees the Future overcast
> With broader gloom than even the Present.
>   (149)

And another poignant moment is also enhanced by repetition:

> Nought pondereth he of wars of yore,
> Of battling Ghibelline and Guelph,
>   And bootless fights and trampled lands,
>   And Gallic swords and Teuton chains
>   (146)

The final poem to be considered in this chapter is "The Nameless One," which was published posthumously on October 27, 1849; but O'Donoghue thinks it belongs to 1842 because Mangan refers to himself as thirty-nine years old. However, as O'Donoghue himself has shown, Mangan, out of vanity, virtually never told his true age; and, as the same biographer admits, 1842 was not a year characterized by the kind of despair evident in "The Nameless One." Consequently, it is difficult to determine how long before his death Mangan wrote this farewell ballad. The poem is a poignant summation of Mangan's life and should be read in its entirety:

> Roll forth, my song, like the rushing river,
>   That sweeps along to the mighty sea;
> God will inspire me while I deliver
>   My soul of thee!
>
> Tell thou the world, when my bones lie whitening
>   Amid the last homes of youth and eld,
> That there was once one whose veins ran lightning
>   No eye beheld.
>
> Tell how his boyhood was one drear night-hour
>   How shone for *him*, through his griefs and gloom,
> No star of all heaven sends to light our
>   Path to the tomb.
>
> Roll on, my song, and to after ages
>   Tell how, disdaining all earth can give,
> He would have taught men, from wisdom's pages,
>   The way to live.

And tell how trampled, derided, hated,
    And worn by weakness, disease, and wrong,
He fled for shelter to God, who mated
        His soul with song —

With Song which alway, sublime or vapid,
    Flowed like a rill in the morning beam,
Perchance not deep, but intense and rapid —
        A mountain stream.

Tell how this Nameless, condemned for years long
    To herd with demons from hell beneath,
Saw things that made him, with groans and tears, long
        For even death.

Go on to tell how, with genius wasted,
    Betrayed in friendship, befooled in love,
With spirit shipwrecked, and young hopes blasted,
        He still, still strove.

Till, spent with toil, dreeing death for others,
    And some whose hands should have wrought for *him*
(If children live not for sires and mothers,)
        His mind grew dim.

And he fell far through that pit abysmal
    The gulf and grave of Maginn and Burns,
And pawned his soul for the devil's dismal
        Stock of returns.

But yet redeemed it in days of darkness,
    And shapes and signs of the final wrath,
When death, in hideous and ghastly starkness,
        Stood on his path.

And tell how now, amid wreck and sorrow,
    And want, and sickness, and houseless nights,
He bides in calmness the silent morrow,
        That no ray lights.

And lives he still, then? Yes! Old and hoary
    At thirty-nine, from despair and woe,
He lives enduring what future story
        Will never know.

> Him grant a grave to, ye pitying noble,
>   Deep in your bosoms! There let him dwell!
> He, too, had tears for all souls in trouble,
>   Here and in hell.
>   (120-22)

Padraic Colum does not think the poem among Mangan's best because it is more rhetoric than poetry. There is no question that the poem includes some rhetoric, but on the whole it is a very impressive work and deserves to be included in the collection of Mangan's best poetry. Moreover, this poem was a favorite of James Joyce, who recited it often in public.[4] There are some interesting insights into Mangan unless we choose, like Sheridan, to discard the autobiographical elements of the poem because it is "not like Mangan" but is simply the fashionable reflection of a pessimistic mood. It is not difficult, nevertheless, to see how closely some of the stanzas reflect Mangan's life. There is the personal element so effectively presented in the fifth stanza where the derided and worn poet "fled for shelter to God, who mated/His soul with song." Likewise, the self-analysis of the following stanza is an accurate account of the poet himself who was "Perchance not deep, but intense and rapid —/A mountain stream."

The seventh stanza is simply the expression of a feeling betrayed countless other times in Mangan's poetry, but its concluding emphasis on his striving in the face of "hopes blasted" is probably, as Sheridan suggests, a pose; and we need not look far for the source of it in this poet who so loved Byron. The ninth stanza is an accurate and characteristically Manganesque description of himself as one who "pawned his soul for the devil's dismal/Stock of returns." The final stanza can be read as a pose only if we see "here and in hell" as referring to his dwelling place, which it obviously does not. But that Mangan had compassion for those who suffered "here and in hell" can be fairly easily accepted from his total canon. It is not, then, clear what Sheridan has in mind in finding the last stanza a fearless pose.

CHAPTER 5

Prose Works

A brief word must be said about a less significant side of Mangan's writings, his prose works. Critical problems surrounding the prose are much greater than those concerning the poetry. As Rudi Holzapfel has pointed out in his bibliography of Mangan's *Dublin University Magazine* writings, Mangan's poetic style is unmistakable in unsigned or pseudonymous poems, but the identification of his prose writing with the same kind of inerrancy is a much more difficult task for the bibliographer.[1] Whatever the problems involved in gathering Mangan's prose, O'Donoghue has left us a volume of such prose writings. They provide a remarkable insight into the poet, especially into the witty, humorous side of a poet who did not show often enough such wit in his better verse. Apart from that, however, O'Donoghue's collection indicates Mangan's genuine ability to tell a story but not to develop it fully. There are twelve selections from Mangan, of which the first two, "The Thirty Flasks" and "The Man in the Cloak," and the last two, "The Three Rings" and "The Story of the Old Wolf," are the best.

The first two stories from the *Dublin University Magazine* of 1838 are rather Faustian. "The Thirty Flasks" tells of a man who exchanges inches of his height for money, but just before he gives the last inch of thirty inches, which would have brought him from six feet to a permanent three-feet-six-inches, he is saved by a legacy. The conclusion is not so satisfactory as the story, and the possibilities in the parable of reducing one's stature through gambling are maintained but not developed so fully as they could be.

In "The Man in the Cloak," Johann Klaus Braunbrock, a German bank clerk, is saved from a life of imprisonment for embezzling funds when he sells his soul to a damned, Irish wanderer called Melmouth or simply The Man in the Cloak. At the theater, this strange wanderer had transformed a play, for Braunbrock's eyes, into a preview of the life that would be his as a result of the embezzlement. Braunbrock agrees to sell his soul to Melmouth for deliverance from capture and for his pipe, a talisman which gives him unlimited power and knowledge. Braunbrock, rescued, begins a seven-year span of self-indulgence as the new Man in the Cloak, at the end of which time he realizes how jaded, unhappy, and especially how alone he is. Like his predecessor, Braunbrock has everything but control of his own destiny. Thus, he begins to look about the world for a new victim who will accept his talisman, assume his role, and enable him to possess once again the charge of his own destiny. He finds such a one, a Frenchman, after much search and after praying with a priest at the funeral of the former Man in the Cloak. To palliate the notion that prayer produced such a victim, the author hurriedly tells us the history of how the pipe, has repeatedly been passed on in turn to others.

The influence of Mangan's hero, Charles Maturin, the Irish Gothic novelist, is evident in the use of Melmouth; but, despite a quick-moving prose style, Mangan does not have staying power. His stories begin with a good idea, often a derivative one, but they fade in the end. What makes "The Man in the Cloak" of some interest, however, is the use of autobiographical elements. Mangan himself wore such a cloak, and his own sense of isolation is the greatest suffering his hero experiences in the story.

"The Three Rings" is a good parable about the Jew, Nathaniel, who is asked by Sal-ad-Deen why he professes a false religion. Nathaniel answers by narrating the story of the man who gave three rings to three sons. The religious point is like that of Swift's *Tale of the Tub* in which the father gives coats to his three sons and asks that they not embellish them. The sons later rationalize their father's explicit will and change their coats to suit each new fashion. The coats represent, of course, the original religion bequeathed to men, which men have embellished with subsequent religious practices of their own choosing. Although Mangan's idea is again derivative, he takes Swift's idea of religious primacy possessed equally by Catholicism, Lutheranism, and Calvinism and extends it to mean, not equal validity of all religions, but the uncertainty of God's favor to any one religion. In Mangan's story there was originally only one true ring guaranteeing God's favor; and this ring was to be bequeathed by each father to his favorite son. When it came to the father who had three equally deserving sons, he had two identical rings made so each son could have one. One son possessed the true ring, or true relationship with God; but none could decipher which it was; and because of their prosecution of one another, the judge could only determine that their selfishness indicated that none of them had a true relationship with God. Thus, the judge could only tell them to practice virtue, pass the rings on to their children, and forecast that perhaps a thousand years of virtuous living on the part of one's ancestors would testify to the genuineness of that owner's ring.

"The Three Rings" appeared in the *Irish Penny Journal* on July 25, 1840; and six weeks later in the same journal appeared "The Story of the Old Wolf," an interesting, Aesop-like fable about the inability of a sinner to repent because others will not believe him. The result is he turns bitter, vicious, and harms society still more. The story, which is very light in touch throughout, surprises with its sudden violence at the end as the wolf destroys the children of shepherds who have refused to make peace with him.

"The Story of the Old Wolf" and "The Three Rings," like "The Man in the Cloak," may indicate something personal about Mangan at this time. He did feel his isolation, and he was ever the public sinner trying to repent and change his habits. Likewise, his religious groping during his thirties can be seen reflected in Nathaniel's statement about the difficulty of knowing the true relationship to God. The stories are, nevertheless, potboilers; and Mangan's literary stature is not enhanced by his prose.

The kind of Romantic tradition that characterized Mangan's prose stories is evident. He wrote to satisfy the popular demands of his day, and even these four best stories in the collection are not remembered for themselves. Mangan's prose does approximately what Browning's plays, or better still the novels of Shaw, do: they provide insight into an artist great in another medium. His stories are not the work of genius, nor are Shaw's novels. Yet immersed in Shaw's pedestrian novels is that sparkling dialogue which was to be properly applied in another medium, the drama. Browning's dramas did show the psychological action in character if they did not show character in action, and they were wedded to the proper medium in the dramatic monologue. In Mangan's prose can be seen the love of wordplay and pun which were to make him a master of rhyme like his model, Byron. Likewise the humor is everywhere present which surprisingly asserts itself in the midst of serious poems from time to time — a characteristic that ties Mangan in, as Chesterton says, with the old Irish tradition of moving from the serious to the humorous and back again.

CHAPTER 6

Influence on Other Writers

NO question exists about Mangan's influence on later writers, particularly of his own country; but the extent of his influence abroad is very difficult to establish. His influence on Joyce and Yeats is readily acknowledged. Whether and how much Poe learned from Mangan is controverted, and the extent to which other American admirers like Henry Wadsworth Longfellow, Herman Melville, and James Ryder Randall were influenced can only be conjectured.

James Joyce was not prone to praise other authors, but Mangan was a hero of his from his undergraduate days. "Joyce was very sparing in his praise of other writers. . . . Except for Ibsen and Dante, the only other author whom he favored was James Clarence Mangan, and I remember the intense pleasure with which all those assembled one night in my father's house heard him recite *The Nameless One* by the hapless Irish poet."[1] In 1902, before beginning work on Stephen Hero, Joyce published his essay on Mangan in *St. Stephen's;* and he is lavish in his praise of the poet:

Mangan, it must be remembered, wrote with no native literary tradition to guide him, and for a public which cared for matters of the day, and for poetry only so far as it might illustrate these. He could not often revise what he wrote, and he has often striven with Moore and Walsh on their own ground. But the best of what he has written makes its appeal surely, because it was conceived by the imagination which he called, I think, the mother of things, whose dreams we are, who imageth us to herself, and to ourselves and imageth herself in us — the power before whose breath the mind in creation is (to use Shelley's image), as a fading coal. Though even in the best of Mangan the presence of alien emotions is sometimes felt, the presence of an imaginative personality reflecting the light of imaginative beauty is more vividly felt. East and West meet in that personality (we know how): images interweave there like soft luminous scarves and words ring like brilliant mail, and whether the song is of Ireland or of Istambol it has the same refrain, a prayer that peace may come again to her who has lost her peace, the moonwhite pearl of his soul, Ameen.[2]

And again in writing of Mangan's ability with sounds, and comparing him with Poe, Joyce says:

The matchless passages which are found in other poems are so good that they could not have been written by anyone but Mangan. He might have written a treatise on the poetical art for he is more cunning in his use of the musical echo than is Poe, the high priest of most modern schools, and there is a mastery, which no school can teach but which obeys an interior command, which we may trace in "Kathaleen Ny-Houlahan," where the refrain changes the trochaic scheme abruptly for a line of firm marching iambs.

All his poetry remembers wrong and suffering and the aspiration of one who has suffered and who is moved to great cries and gestures when that sorrowful hour rushes upon the heart. This is the theme of a hundred songs but of none so intense as these songs which are made in noble misery, as his favorite Swedenborg would say, out of the vastation of soul.[3]

Joyce's enthusiasm for Mangan became an evangelical cause which extended beyond his undergraduate days. Years later he tried to bring Mangan to the attention of the Italians.[4] The love of Mangan was decidedly literary and not national. Joyce was not nationalistic and neither was Mangan basically, only lending himself to Ireland's cause in his later years. Moreover, this later nationalism was the only side of Mangan with which Joyce was not in sympathy.

So much, however, for what Joyce said and thought of Mangan. The question still remains as to what literary influence from Mangan might be evident in Joyce's work; and part of the answer has been well demonstrated by Marvin Magalaner. Many of the traits of Stephen Hero, Stephen Dedalus, and also the aloof Leopold Bloom are probably taken from the fragment of Mangan's autobiography. There is much evidence in Joyce's article that he had read Mangan's autobiography, as in Joyce's use of the phrase "boa constrictor" which Mangan there applies to his father. But, if Joyce had not seen Mangan's autobiography when the account of his hero was published in 1902, he certainly knew the essential details of Mangan's life.[5]

Professor Magalaner thinks that the concept of the artist's bearing the stigma of vision and the defensive reserve of the artist are evident in Joyce's heroes because they are patterned heavily on Mangan himself. Even Stephen's father is as much like Mangan's father as he is like Joyce's. Many of Mangan's own somewhat exaggerated remarks in the autobiography come from what he imbibed from his boyhood hero, Byron. And, in speaking of this Byronic pose evident in Mangan's autobiography, it is interesting to note that Stephen is ridiculed in *A Portrait of the Artist as a Young Man* for his championing of Byron. Also, as Magalaner has noted, the young girl whom Stephen loves in "Araby" is "Mangan's sister." Perhaps nothing can be made of this last fact more than Joyce's absorption with the poet while writing these works.

To establish a stylistic influence of Mangan on Joyce is certainly beyond the scope of this brief book. Did the incredible music of this tragic poet have its effect upon Joyce's sensitive ear? Did he help make Joyce conscious of sound? Did Mangan's fondness for puns play any part in *Finnegan's Wake?* An affirmative answer cannot even be suggested without much more study of the Joyce canon for possible influences from his Irish predecessor. The most that can be said at present is that, in writing his undergraduate essay on the essence of poetry, Joyce chose Mangan as his exemplar.

The influence on Yeats is in one way less obvious, less direct; but the reader may notice more obvious affinities between the two national poets. Like Joyce, Yeats also wrote an essay on Mangan — in fact, two essays. The first appeared in *The Irish Fireside* in March, 1887, an article in which he furnished a flattering biographical sketch of his predecessor and indicated that he had learned from Mangan the need for a nonpolitical tradition in poetry.[6] The other was an article written for *United Ireland* on August 22, 1891, entitled "Clarence Mangan's Love Affairs." Although it repeats much in the previous article, this essay praises Mangan's genius and says of the troublesome time that Mangan had with his fellow clerks, "If you tie a red ribbon to the leg of a seagull the other gulls will pick it to death. To the soul of Clarence Mangan was tied the burning ribbon of genius."[7]

Perhaps more important than the two essays was the edition of *Poems and Ballads of Young Ireland* which Yeats helped publish in 1888. These Young Ireland poets, of whom Mangan was the most prestigious, were a decided influence on the young William Butler Yeats, as Richard Ellmann shows.[8] They began the modern national movement in Irish letters, and Yeats felt a strong affinity and admiration for them, as well as a desire to surpass their efforts. From Mangan, Yeats may have taken many of his national themes, such as that in Maud Gonne's favorite poem, "Red Hanrahan's Song About Ireland."[9] The form, as well as the idea, of the poem is very like Mangan's "Kathaleen Ny-Houlahan" — if we compare the opening stanza of each. First Mangan's:

> Long they pine in weary woe, the nobles of our land,
> Long they wander to and fro, proscribed, alas! and banned;
> Feastless, houseless, altarless, they bear the exile's brand,
>   But their hope is in the coming-to of Kathaleen Ny-Houlahan!
>   (16)

Then Yeats's:

> The old brown thorn-trees break in two high over Cummen Strand,
> Under a bitter black wind that blows from the left hand;
> Our courage breaks like an old tree in a black wind and dies,
> But we have hidden in our hearts the flame out of the eyes
> Of Cathleen, the daughter of Houlihan.[10]

The similarity in theme is obvious, and the seven-beat line is utilized by Yeats as well as by Mangan. The use of refrain, with the standard, Manganesque slight change or incremental repetition is used by Yeats so that "Of Cathleen" becomes "Is Cathleen" by the last stanza. Mangan used a four-line stanza in which the final line was longer, adding emphasis to the refrain. Yeats, using a variation of this form, extended the stanza to a short fifth line in which the refrain stood by itself.

Jeffares suggests that the destructive force of the wind in "Leda and the Swan" is something Yeats came to via Mangan's fine poem "Gone in the Wind." However, it is not the purpose here to scan the Yeats canon to establish the influence of Mangan. One cannot read the work of the chief poet of "Young Ireland" and then that of the poet who brought Irish poetry to fruition without being aware of at least the implicit debt Yeats owed his predecessor. Yeats acknowledged this indebtedness but he thought himself less narrow in interest than any of his Irish predecessors. He thought of his nationalistic verse as transcending mere topicality and as having a universality that the poetry of the Young Ireland writers did not have. While this might be true generally of the Young Ireland writers, it has already been sufficiently pointed out that Mangan was not nationalistic in any narrow sense. He was apolitical; he wrote for political journals in which he reflected none of the concerns of his editors; and he wrote explicitly nationalistic verse only in his later years. Furthermore, Mangan's Irish verse, like his Oriental verse, has its own universality. No one who knows Mangan's life or work thinks for a moment that the imaginative picture of a country's suffering, devastation, and awaited deliverance is merely patriotic; for he depicts poignantly the suffering human soul and does so with little of the questionable sincerity of his favorite, Byron.

Mangan's influence within his own country cannot, of course, be summed up by speaking of that influence on Joyce and Yeats. We can understand the Irish renaissance of the 1890's only by seeing it as a reenkindling of that other national and literary rebirth of the 1840's, that spearheaded by Young Ireland and its paper, *The Nation.* As the central literary figure in this scholarly and patriotic group, Mangan was the prime "translator" of older Irish poetry and earlier national themes. He thus fathered the movement that came to fruition with Yeats, John Synge, George Russell, Sean O'Casey, and the Abbey Theater. Young Ireland died with its unsuccessful insurrection in 1848, and Mangan himself died the following year, but Yeats picked up the nationalistic torch dropped by Young Ireland and its chief poet when he became interested in Mangan and wrote of him at the outset of his own career as a professional poet in 1887 and when he edited the *Poems and Ballads of Young Ireland* in 1888. Thus through Yeats most explicitly Mangan became the chief progenitor of the whole literary rebirth in Ireland.

The influence of Mangan on Poe has already been mentioned in passing. The two men had obviously suggestive similarities in life as well as in their work, and Mangan has been called the "Irish Poe." They were close to being exact contemporaries; Poe was six years younger but died, like Mangan, in 1849. Also, like Mangan, he was disappointed in finding his sweetheart engaged to another, he drank heavily, he was a good conversationalist when under the influence of alcohol, he had difficulty holding a job because of drink, he may have been addicted to drugs, and he died a victim of his own indulgence.

Stylistically, the men are perhaps even more similar. Both had an incredible ear, both used rhythm and refrain in the same peculiar but effective way, and both employed much repetition and internal rhyme. Likewise, both made much use of anapests and the trisyllabic foot. Besides similarities of form, the melancholy tone and the love of the grotesque are also common to both.

Since there are so many obvious affinities, the argument has been advanced that Poe learned from the Irish poet whom he probably read in the *Dublin University Magazine*. The argument points out that the earmark of Mangan's poetry, the refrain, is something he obviously used before Poe. The American poet Louise Imogen Guiney demonstrated that the haunting repetition of sweet sounds to be found in "The Raven" (1845) and "Ululame" (1847) came late in Poe's career, long after Mangan's use of such sound (as early as 1839). She also indicates that, when Lenore was first published in 1843, it did not have "a single touch of the repetitions which now give it such memorable glamour; the repetitions were superadded later and on second thought. Now Mangan from 1839 and 1840 on bestowed on almost everything he wrote the curious involved diction in question." Furthermore, she continues, "In the *Dublin University Magazine*, during the years when Poe was attaining his zenith of success, figure successive specimens of the unchanged art of the man who had the start of him by at least five years; for *The Barmecides* was in print in 1839, and *The Karamanian Exile*, a finished model of its kind, was contemporary with the as yet cisatlantic *Raven*, and the predecessor of *Ululame, Lenore, Eulalie, For Annie*, and the rest."[11]

It is possible that Poe might have read Mangan in the *Dublin University Magazine* without recognizing him under the various aliases that Mangan used, as Thompson points out; but, unlike Padraic Colum, Louise Imogen Guiney, Thomas MacDonagh, and countless others, Thompson thinks that, if there were an influence, it was probably Poe who influenced Mangan. To support his idea, Thompson uses the 1827 edition of *Al Aaraaf, Tamerlane and Other Poems* to demonstrate possible influence.

The most extensive study of the problem of the Poe-Mangan influence was done in a 1929 doctoral dissertation by Henry Edward Cain, who summarized his conclusions: "The statement that Poe was a student of Mangan has no foundation in fact. The evidence rather indicates that neither poet was influenced by the other. Apart from some similiarities in the technique of the two men, there is no direct or indirect evidence to support the contention that one influenced the other. On the other hand, it has been pointed out that both men had a common source in Coleridge, and that both were ardent students of Byron."[12] Cain's summary is a reasonable one, for no evidence exists to prove that Poe was influenced by Mangan either consciously or unconsciously. They had many stylistic similarities, and Poe seems to have come to these qualities of style slightly later than Mangan.

But, even if priority is established, influence is not, and on the evidence uncovered so far, it would be rash to make some of the claims that have been made for Mangan.

Another poet, Henry Wadsworth Longfellow, was very much moved in 1843 by reading Mangan's "translations" from the German. He did not recognize the author, but he wrote to his friend Ferdinand Freilgrath, "Have you seen the translations from your poems in the *Dublin University Magazine?* They are not very literal, but exceedingly spirited, and excite a good deal of commendation from all readers." Unfortunately, we do not know what Freilgrath thought of Mangan's free and personal "translations" of his work, but Longfellow thought highly enough of Mangan's artistry to include about ten of these translations in his *The Poets and Poetry of Europe* (1845).[13]

As we mentioned earlier, in speaking of "The Karamanian Exile," James Ryder Randall was an enthusiastic reader of Mangan. The editor of the *New Orleans Delta,* Joseph Brenan, had encouraged his young reporter's poetry by giving a copy of Mangan's works to Randall. And Randall himself indicated how "Maryland, My Maryland" was formed in his mind while reading "The Karamanian Exile." He completed the poem, in fact, shortly after turning to Mangan's poem and finding his meter.[14]

Finally, Thompson has shown the influence of Mangan on the poetry of Melville. "The Time of the Barmecides" seems to have been the American's favorite, and he flattered Mangan by his "The Age of the Antonines." Likewise, Thompson indicates the similarity between other Mangan and Melville poems. Incidentally, Melville's copy of Mangan's poems is well annotated and can be found in the Harvard University Library.[15]

How many more writers the prolific Mangan has influenced is impossible to say. However, the seminal role he enjoyed in the Irish Renaissance made him a forceful influence on the most significant body of writing in twentieth-century English letters. But, whatever Mangan's influence on other writers, his reputation will continue to depend upon his poetry. That reputation, of course, has not done as well as that of some of his Romantic contemporaries — even minor figures like Beddoes and Clare; and this study is not going to conclude by making grandiose claims for a minor poet. Yet this extraordinarily prolific poet has a solid core of poems, perhaps thirty or forty of which have an immortality about them. Thirty or forty poems may not seem many among some eight hundred, but Matthew Arnold could discard the vast majority of Wordsworth's canon and on the basis of a solid few call Wordsworth the third greatest poet in the language. Mangan's life should justify a good many more potboilers than Wordsworth's life. And while there are no *Intimations Odes* in Mangan's canon, there is that core, that solid body of immortal works on which the final judgment of his genius should be based.

Notes and References

Preface

1. Mangan produced many of his poems under various *noms de plume* so that he might avoid the strictures against one name appearing three times in the same issue; and this practice has made the collecting and the editing of Mangan's work most difficult. Estimates as to how many poems he really published range from Mitchel's approximately two hundred and forty, through O'Donoghue's figure of eight hundred, to Louise Imogen Guiney's estimate of two thousand. O'Donoghue has collected what he thinks are the best and least ephemeral among Mangan's poems, and his edition includes about two hundred poems. Of the two hundred edited by O'Donoghue, there are approximately thirty-five or forty which seem to me to be outstanding. Although this percentage may seem small, we should consider the question of how many poets have produced as many really good works. Like Keats, Mangan was an infallible judge of his work: he knew what was good and what was not. In the few instances where he had a chance to revise, the revision was always a decided improvement; and the pity is that he did not live to revise his poems for a collected edition.

Chapter One

1. Marvin Magalaner, "Mangan and Joyce's Dedalus Family," *Philological Quarterly,* XXXI (1952), 363-71. James Joyce may have had the elder Mangan, as well as his own father, in mind in his portrait of Simon Dedalus.

2. James Kilroy, ed., *The Autobiography of James Clarence Mangan* (Dublin, 1968), pp. 13-14. References to the *Autobiography* are to this newest text which has been edited from the original manuscript.

3. D. J. O'Donoghue, *The Life and Writings of James Clarence Mangan* (Chicago, 1897), p. 4, p. 13, and *passim.* Subsequent references to the *Life* are to this most complete text.

4. James Joyce, "James Clarence Mangan," *St. Stephen's* (May, 1902), p. 6. This work has limited circulation; however, the article may also be found in the *James Joyce Review,* I (1957), 31-38.

5. *Autobiography,* p. 18.

6. Joyce, p. 6.

7. G. K. Chesterton, "A Chapter in Irish Poetry," *Speaker* (October 31, 1903), pp. 115-16.

8. Sir Charles Gavan Duffy, "Personal Memoirs of James Clarence Mangan," *Dublin Review,* CXLII (1908), 278-94.

9. O'Donoghue, *Life,* p. 145.

10. Louise Imogen Guiney, *James Clarence Mangan: His Selected Poems* (Boston, 1897), pp. 19ff.

11. John Mitchel, ed., *Poems by James Clarence Mangan* (New York, 1866), p. 14.

12. *Autobiography,* p. 17.

13. O'Donoghue, *Life,* p. 7.

14. Guiney, pp. 24-25.

15. O'Donoghue tells us he contributed nothing for five years. More recently, Holzapfel contends there is proof he did write for the journals in 1826, in 1831, and probably in 1830, leaving a hiatus of only two years. See. R. P. Holzapfel, "Mangan's Poetry in the *Dublin University Magazine:* A Bibliography," *Hermathena,* CV (Autumn, 1967), 40-54.

16. M. Whitcomb Hess, "James Clarence Mangan: A Story of Triumph," *Catholic World,* CLXIX (June, 1949), 185-90. Hess, who makes a hagiography of his life, laments only that Mangan did not know St. Thomas Aquinas as well as he knew Kant or he would not have suffered as he did from "hypochondriasis."

17. *Autobiography,* p. 28.

18. Charles B. Quinn, "Twenty Gaelic Poems Translated by James Clarence Mangan," Unpublished doctoral dissertation, Fordham University, 1960, p. xiv.

19. Mitchel, pp. 11-12.

20. O'Donoghue, *Life,* p. 60.

21. Duffy, p. 285.

22. Guiney, p. 17.

23. Guiney and Justin McCarthy, ed., *Irish Literature* (Philadelphia, 1904), VI, 2350-52, date his work for Trinity Library from this period; O'Donoghue assigns it to a period ten years later.

24. O'Donoghue, *Life,* p. 112.

25. Duffy, p. 290.

26. Mitchel, p. 20.

Chapter Two

1. Justin McCarthy, 2350-52, is one of the few critics who believe Mangan might have known some of these Oriental languages.

2. D. J. O'Donoghue, *Poems of James Clarence Mangan* (Dublin, 1903), p. 183. All subsequent citations of Mangan's poetry are from this edition and are referred to in the text by page.

3. Mitchel. p. 20.

4. O'Donoghue, *Life,* pp. 119-20.

5. *Ibid.,* pp. 41-42.

6. Padraic Colum, "James Clarence Mangan," *Dublin Magazine,* VIII (1933), 33-34.

7. Francis J. Thompson, "Mangan in America: 1850 - 1860," *Dublin Magazine,* XXVII (1952), 39. Also in Guiney, pp. 359-60.

8. Colum, p. 32.

9. Chesterton, p. 116.

10. Friedrich Rückert, *Poetische Werke* (Sauerlander Verlag: Frankfurt, 1868), III, 56.

Chapter Three

1. Quinn, p. 72

2. Colum, p. 38.

3. Patrick C. Power, *A Literary History of Ireland* (Cork, 1969), p. 97.

4. Colum, p. 36.

5. *Ibid.,* p. 38.

6. *Ibid.,* p. 39.

7. Quinn, p. 37.

8. James Kilroy, *James Clarence Mangan* (Lewisburg, 1970), p. 51.

9. Guiney, p. 344.

10. Kilroy, p. 41.

Chapter Four

1. Hess, 185-90, as mentioned earlier. Also O'Donoghue's biography plays upon the same theme throughout.

2. O'Donoghue, *Life,* p. 137.

3. *Ibid., p. 183.*

4. *Robert Scholes and Richard M. Kain, eds., The Workshop of Daedalus* (Evanston, 1965), p. 153.

Chapter Five

1. Holzapfel, "Mangan's Poetry in the *Dublin University Magazine:* A Bibliography," pp. 40-41.

Chapter Six

1. Scholes and Kain, *The Workshop of Daedalus,* p. 178.

2. Joyce, pp. 8-9.

3. *Ibid.,* p. 10.

4. Richard Ellmann, *James Joyce* (New York, 1959), p. 99.

5. Magalaner, pp. 363-71.

6. W. B. Yeats, "Clarence Mangan," *Uncollected Prose by W. B. Yeats,* ed. John P. Frayne (New York, 1970), I, 114-19.

7. *Ibid.,* pp. 194-98.

8. Richard Ellmann, *The Identity of Yeats* (New York, 1964), p. 12.

9. A. Norman Jeffares, *W. B. Yeats: Man and Poet* (New York, 1966), pp. 138-39.

10. W. B. Yeats, *The Collected Poems* (New York, 1959), p. 79.

11. Guiney, pp. 106-07.

12. Henry E. Cain, "James Clarence Mangan and the Poe-Mangan Question," Unpublished Doctoral Dissertation, Catholic University, 1929, p. 93.

13. Thompson, pp. 30-41.

14. Guiney, pp. 359-60.

15. R. P. Holzapfel, *James Clarence Mangan: A Checklist of Printed and Other Sources* (Dublin, 1969), p. 75.

Selected Bibliography

PRIMARY SOURCES

Anthologia Germanica. 2 vols. Dublin: Curry, 1845.

The Poets and Poetry of Munster: A Selection of Irish Songs with Poetical Translations by James Clarence Mangan. Dublin: J. O'Daly, 1849.

Poems. Edited and with Biographical Introduction by John Mitchel. New York: D. & J. Sadlier, 1866.

James Clarence Mangan: His Selected Poems. Edited and with a Study by L. I. Guiney. Boston: Lamson-Wolfe, 1897.

Poems. Centenary edition with Preface and Notes by D. J. O'Donoghue. Dublin: O'Donoghue & Co., 1903.

The Prose Writings. Centenary edition by D. J. O'Donoghue with Essay by Lionel Johnson. Dublin: O'Donoghue and Co., 1904.

Autobiography. Edited from the MS. by James Kilroy. Dublin: Dolmen, 1968. This fragment first published in *Poets and Poetry of Munster* above.

SECONDARY SOURCES

1. Biography and Criticism

CAIN, HENRY E. "James Clarence Mangan and the Poe-Mangan Question." Unpublished doctoral dissertation, Catholic Univ., 1929. The most complete study of the problem of priority and influence. Decides for a common source.

CHESTERTON, G. K. "A Chapter in Irish Poetry." *Speaker* (October 31, 1903), pp. 115-16. Short review with some typically perceptive insights from Chesterton; on the whole, deals more with Ireland than with Mangan.

COLUM, PADRAIC. "James Clarence Mangan." *The Dublin Magazine,* VIII (April-June, 1933), 32-40. Interesting insight by this gifted younger poet and playwright of the Irish Renaissance into ancestor of movement. Unlike Yeats, does not think highly of "The Nameless One." Thinks Mangan's great poetry amounts to about fifteen poems, which he names.

Duffy, Sir Charles Gavan. "Personal Memoirs of James Clarence Mangan." Dublin Review, CXLII (1908), 278-94. Leader of *The Nation* and of Young Ireland gives personal recollections and corrects some statements of Mitchel's. Perversely believes Mangan when he denies opium addiction.

Hess, M. Whitcomb, "James Clarence Mangan: A Story of Triumph." *Catholic World*, CLXIX (June, 1949), 185-90. Interesting comparison with Kierkegaard; but generally too pious a view of Mangan's problems.

Holzapfel, R. P. *James Clarence Mangan: A Checklist of Printed and Other Sources.* Dublin: Scepter, 1969. Very helpful book for Mangan scholars. Includes all books by Mangan and all editions of his poetry and prose; all books in which he had a hand, all important books and articles mentioning him at any length; even unpublished theses and works in progress.

———. "Mangan's Poetry in the *Dublin University Magazine: A Bibliography.*" Hermathena, CV (Autumn, 1967), 40-54. Good and useful essay as well as bibliography; corrects O'Donoghue's notion that Mangan "wrote little and published nothing" between 1826 and 1831.

Joyce, James. "James Clarence Mangan." *St. Stephen's* (May, 1902), pp. 1-16. Joyce's undergraduate paper on Mangan; shows a devotion that lasted a lifetime. Helpful for understanding of Mangan's relationship with his father. The article also appears in the *James Joyce Review,* I (1957), 31-38.

Kilroy, James. *James Clarence Mangan.* Lewisburg: Bucknell Univ. Press, 1970. Brief, well-written monograph by the editor of Mangan's *Autobiography.* Perhaps the most useful place to begin a study of the poet.

Magalaner, Marvin. "Mangan and Joyce's Dedalus Family." *P. Q.,* XXXI (1952), 363-71. Article shows that *The Portrait of the Artist* is not all autobiography, and that Joyce used facts from his boyhood idol, Mangan, and from Mangan's family as readily as he did from his own.

Nevinson, Henry. "The Dark Rosaleen." *North American Review,* CCIX (1904), 252-62. Article is more political and social than literary. Nevinson thinks that most popular poem of Mangan's is his only perfect poem. Article very negative toward rest of Mangan's poetry, and only enhances already exaggerated place of this poem in Mangan's total canon.

O'Donoghue, D. J. *The Life and Writings of James Clarence Mangan.* Chicago: P. V. Fitzpatrick, 1897. Best and most complete biography. However, like Hess article above, it too stresses Mangan's always remaining a "good Catholic" despite Mitchel and others pointing out that Mangan's middle years were devoted to the occult.

Quinn, Charles B. "Twenty Gaelic Poems Translated by James Clarence Mangan." Unpublished doctoral dissertation, Fordham, Univ., 1960.

Helpful introduction and study of Mangan's knowledge of Irish. Shows by comparison with the Irish text how original and personal Mangan's Irish translations are.

SHERIDAN, DESMOND. *James Clarence Mangan*. Dublin: Talbot, 1937. Interesting and readable biography; adds little to O'Donoghue, which will be the case with subsequent biographers until there is a real breakthrough of new information.

THOMPSON, FRANCIS J. "Mangan in America: 1850 - 1860." *Dublin Magazine,* XXVII (1952), 30-41. Discusses influence on Longfellow, Randall, Melville, *et al.*

———. "Poe and Mangan." *Dublin Magazine,* XXV (1950), 33-40. Opposed to Guiney, MacDonagh, *et al,* who contend for Mangan's influence on Poe.

WYNNE, MICHAEL. "The Face of Mangan." *Hermathena,* CV (Autumn, 1967), 55-59. Discusses some of the various portraits of Mangan; includes Sir Frederic Burton's death-bed portrait and the silhouette belonging to Father Meehan.

YEATS, WILLIAM BUTLER. "Clarence Mangan." *Uncollected Prose by W. B. Yeats.* Collected and edited by John P. Frayne. New York: Columbia Univ., 1970, I, 114-19. Biographical sketch, depends on Mitchel and Duffy, but interesting insights from a kindred spirit. Original article in *Irish Fireside* on March 12, 1887.

———. "Clarence Mangan's Love Affair." *Uncollected Prose by W. B. Yeats,* I, 194-98. Repeats much of earlier article, but adds a few sensible and penetrating points, particularly helpful in understanding contradictory reports about effect of Mangan's father and fellow employees upon him. Article a reprint of one originally appearing in *United Ireland,* August 22, 1891.

2. *Historical Background*

ALSPACH, RUSSELL K. *Irish Poetry from the English Invasion to 1798.* Philadelphia: University of Pennsylvania Press, 1960. Helpful, well-written work, but meaning by "Irish" poetry only work written in English; Gaelic writers not dealt with.

BECKETT, J. C. *A Short History of Ireland.* 4th ed., 1952; rpt. New York: Harper and Row, 1968. Fine short history; maintains perhaps a little more objectivity than Chauvirer in discussing Ireland's problems with England.

CHAUVIRER, R. C. *A Short History of Ireland.* 2nd ed., 1956; rpt. New York: Mentor-Devon Adair, 1965. Fine short history written by a Frenchman in a lively, somewhat more impassioned style than Beckett.

deBLACAM, AODH. *A First Book of Irish Literature.* Port Washington: Kennikat Press, 1934. Helpful, but capsulelike treatment of all Irish literature, in both Gaelic and English, from the beginning until the twentieth century.

HYDE, DOUGLAS. *A Literary History of Ireland.* New ed. New York: Barnes and Noble, 1967. Excellent coverage of Irish writers through the eighteenth century by the founder of the Gaelic League and first President of Ireland. Treats no Irish writers who wrote in English; should be supplemented by Alspach.

MACDONAGH, OLIVER. *Ireland.* Englewood Cliffs, N.J.: Prentice Hall, 1968. Scholarly study of forces of modern Irish nationalism.

O'CONNOR, FRANK. *A Short History of Irish Literature.* New York: Capricorn, 1968. Sketchier, more impressionistic treatment than Hyde's; filled with insights and opinions of a first-rate writer and translator.

POWER, PATRICK. *A Literary History of Ireland.* Cork: Mercier, 1969. Fine, readable introduction; covers both Gaelic and English literature of Ireland. Beginner would do well to read Power, then O'Connor.

Index

Aird-rinn, 72
Aisling, 64, 69

Bardic schools, 72
Blake, John, 26
Boyne, Battle of, 86
Brian Boru, 83
Browning, Robert, 121
Byron, Lord, 24, 25

Cain, Henry Edward, 127
Caoine, See Keen
Chesterton, G. K., 18, 50, 92, 121
Chichester, Lord, 73
Cuchulain, 81
Clontarf, Battle of, 84
Coleridge, Samuel Taylor, 18, 24, 72
Colum, Padraic, 26, 33, 64, 72, 73, 74,
    118, 127
Columkill, St., 93
Comet, The, 20-21
Courtney, Michael, 16
Cromwell, Oliver, 86

Davis, Thomas, 26
Debide, 72
De Quincey, Thomas, 18
Drogheda, Cromwell's slaughter of in-
    habitants, 86
Druids, 93
Dublin University Magazine, 28, 46
Duffy, Sir Charles Gavan, 18, 22, 25, 26,
    27

Elizabeth, Queen, 69
Ellmann, Richard, 124

Essex, Earl of, 61

Fergusson, Sir Samuel, 26, 69
Filid, 72
"Flight of the Earls," 73

Graham, Father, 16
Guiney, Louise Imogen, 18, 22, 73, 80,
    92, 127

Hayes, Catherine, 21, 30, 98-99
Holzapfel, Rudi, 119
Hopkins, Gerard Manley, 72

James II, King, 86
Jeffares, A. Norman, 125
Joyce, James, 17, 26, 118, 122, 123, 124

Keen, 79
Kenrick, Father, 17
Kilroy, James, 58, 90, 92
Kinsale, Battle of, 61

Longfellow, Henry Wadsworth, 122, 128

MacDonagh, Thomas, 127
Maeve, Queen, 81
Magalaner, Marvin, 123
Mangan, James Clarence, alcoholism
    and drug addiction, 18-19, 26; am-
    bivalence between vulnerable and
    aggressive, 24; as breadwinner, 17-18;
    as Catholic, 20; Autobiography, 16,
    17; becomes member of "Comet
    Club," 20; becomes national poet,
    110; begins Oriental and German

translations, 23; birth, 15; burial, 28; contributes to *Dublin University Magazine,* 23; contributes to *Satirist,* 23; education, 16-17; element of disappointment in love in later poetry, 22; final sickness and death, 28; frequents Phoenix tavern and Star and Garter, 24; German translations, 48; gets job as assistant cataloguer in Trinity College Library, 27; his complaints defended by James Joyce, 17; home life, 15-16; hudibrastic rhyme effectively used, 81; hudibrastic rhyme poorly used, 66, 114; influenced by Swedenborg, 20; influenced by other writers, 24; knowledge of Irish, 60; leaves *The Comet,* 23; love for Margaret Stackpoole, 21-22, 101; love of puns, 25-26; memorizes Shakespeare and Byron, 18; occult reading, 20; odd appearance, 24; Oriental translations, 30; Platonism, 102; political influences, 27; relationship with father and mother, 15; religious search, 20, 99-102, 113-14; sense of isolation, 19; starts publishing poetry, 18; temporary blindness, 19; transcends nationalism, 39; translation question, 29; work in attorney's office, 19; work in scrivener's office, 17

WORKS:
"Advice," 45-46
"And Then No More," 58-59
Anthologia Germanica, 27
"Cean Salla," 65-66
"Coming Event, The," 103-104
"Counsel of a Cosmopolitan," 113-14
"Dark Rosaleen," 27-28, 60-65, 74, 110
"Dream of John MacDonnell, The," 28, 64, 66-69, 110
"Elegiac Verses on the Death of a Beloved Friend," *See* "Lines on the Death of a Beloved Friend"
"Ellen Bawn," 91-92
"Farewell to Patrick Sarsfield, Earl of Lucan, A," 85-89
"Gasparo Bandollo," 15, 114-16
"Genius," 25, 97

"Gone in the Wind," 56-58, 125
"Howling Song of Al Mohara, The," 40-42
"Invitation, An," 113
"Karamanian Exile, The," 30-33, 127, 128
"Kathaleen Ny-Houlahan," 26, 81-83, 125
"Khidder," 105-10
"Kincora," *See* "Lamentation of MacLiag for Kincora"
"Lament for Banba," 89-91
"Lament for the Princess of Tyrone and Tyrconnell (Buried in Rome)," 26, 73-80
"Lamentation of MacLiag for Kincora," 83
"Lamii's Apology for His Nonsense," 39
"Last Words of Al-Hassan, The," 44
"Life and Its Illusions," 102-103
"Lines on the Death of a Beloved Friend," 21, 30, 98
"Man in the Cloak, The," 25, 119-20
"Nameless One, The," 116-18, 122
"O'Hussey's Ode to the Maguire," 26, 28, 69-73, 74, 110
"One Mystery, The," 99-100
"Ride Round the Parapet, The," 50-56
"St. Patrick's Hymn Before Tara," 46, 92-96
"Sayings of Djelim," 39-40
"Story of the Old Wolf, The," 119, 121
"Thirty Flasks, The," 25, 119
"Three Rings, The," 119, 120-21
"Time Ere the Roses Were Blowing, The," 47-48
"Time of the Barmecides, The," 25, 34-36, 127
"Time of the Roses, The," 36-39
"Twenty Golden Years Ago," 48-50
"Vision of Connaught in the Thirteenth Century, A," 24, 28, 110-13
"Wail and Warning of the Three Khalendeers, The," 42-44
"Woman of Three Cows, The," 26, 80-81
"Worst Loss, The," 46

Maturin, Charles, 120
Meehan, Father, 16
Melville, Herman, 122, 128
Mitchel, John, 19, 21-22
Monasticism in Ireland, 93
Mountjoy, Lord, 61, 72

Nation, The, 25, 26, 45

O'Connell, Daniel, 110
O'Connell, John, 26
O'Curry, Eugene, 20-21
O'Daly, Angus, 72
O'Donnell, Hugh Roe, 60-61, 65
O'Donnell, Rory, 73
O'Donoghue, Dennis J., 16, 17, 22, 44, 104, 116
O'Donovan, John, 21
O'Neill, Hugh, 61, 69, 73
O'Rahilly, Egan, 89

Patrick, St., 93
Petrie, George, 20, 25
"Plantations" policy, 69
Poe, Edgar Allen, 33, 42, 122, 126, 128
Power, Patrick, 64
Pretender, Old, 82
Pretender, Young, 68, 82

Randall, James Ryder, 33, 122, 128
"Roisin Dubh," *See* Mangan, "Dark Rosaleen"
Rückert, Friedrich, 27, 30, 55

Sarsfield, Patrick, 73, 86
Selber (Mangan's pseudonym), 30, 48, 103
Shaw, George Bernard, 121
Sheehan, John, 23
Sheridan, Desmond, 18, 22, 118
Speranza, 26

Táin Bó Cúailnge, 81

Ubi Sunt Tradition, 56

Vikings in Ireland, 83-84

Wexford, Cromwell's slaughter of inhabitants, 86
"Wild Geese," 73, 86
Williams, Richard D'Alton, 26

Yeats, William Butler, 26, 81, 122, 124-26
"Young Ireland," 25, 26, 28, 110, 125-26
"Young Italy," 27